St Mary Redcliffe, Bristol
The church and its people

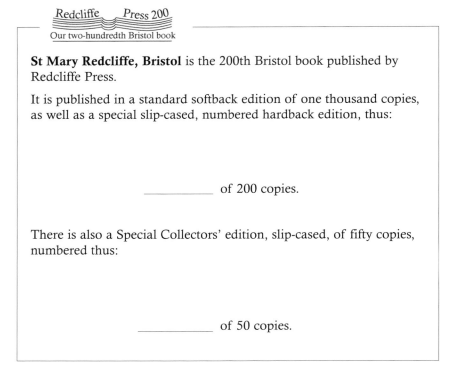

Redcliffe Press 200
Our two-hundredth Bristol book

St Mary Redcliffe, Bristol is the 200th Bristol book published by Redcliffe Press.

It is published in a standard softback edition of one thousand copies, as well as a special slip-cased, numbered hardback edition, thus:

_____ of 200 copies.

There is also a Special Collectors' edition, slip-cased, of fifty copies, numbered thus:

_____ of 50 copies.

Dedicated to John and Sue Pickard

First published in 2008 by Redcliffe Press Ltd., 81g Pembroke Road, Bristol BS8 3EA
www.redcliffepress.co.uk

ISBN 978-1-904537-83-0 softback
ISBN 978-1-906593-03-2 hardback
ISBN 978-1-906593-04-9 collectors' edition

© text: Peter Aughton; new photographs: John Pickard

British Library Cataloguing-in-Publication Data
A catalogue record for this book is available from the British Library

Designed and typeset by Stephen Morris Communications, smc@freeuk.com www.stephen-morris.co.uk
Printed and bound in the UK by The Charlesworth Group, Wakefield

St Mary Redcliffe, Bristol
The church and its people

Peter Aughton

Contents

James Johnson, *View from the north porch to the south porch*, 1828, watercolour, Bristol Museums and Art Gallery (M1947)

Foreword

This book originated from St Mary Redcliffe's Conservation Plan, a work that attempted to look to the past and the future through the architecture of the building. To the past, to see how St Mary Redcliffe became the church it is today; to the future, to see where it might go next. I am grateful to Peter Aughton for the care and attention he gave to this dual aspect as he turned it into this book.

St Mary Redcliffe is a living church. Like all living things it has changed and grown through its life. Three key areas have kept this church alive. The first is the people who have worshipped there and supported it by their involvement in its life. The prayers, care and energy offered over centuries enabled the church to be a living presence.

The second area concerns the community. St Mary Redcliffe has ministered to the people of Redcliffe and they shaped the church. Seafaring, industry, commerce and residents – all made their impact. The life of the city is reflected strongly in the life of the church.

Both of these continue to affect St Mary Redcliffe now and will do so into the future. Those worshipping at the church come from all across the city and all bring new concerns, interests, and prayers together with care, attention and energy. The communities have changed and are changing. A great deal of building is going on around the church. New homes and businesses are being built and there are great plans for re-modelling the space to the north of the church. The church too is changing: our first Parish Missioner has been appointed to lead our outreach. New challenges and opportunities are arising which are being actively pursued. It is the excitement of being alive.

And all depends upon the third and final factor – the living God himself. St Mary Redcliffe exists to bear witness to the life of God in our world, a task which every generation must renew. Our mission is 'O worship the Lord in the beauty of holiness' – an invitation to join with us as we worship God and seek to follow him wherever he will lead us.

The Revd Dr Simon Taylor, Priest-in-Charge, April 2008.

Introduction

It was in the summer of 2005 that our neighbours, John and Sue Pickard, invited my wife and me over for coffee one morning. As we chatted John showed me two very impressive documents on the conservation plan for St Mary Redcliffe. As I was browsing through them John asked me if I would be interested in writing a history of the church.

I was delighted to be asked, but through the window I could see the 'For Sale' notice in our front garden. We were leaving Bristol after nearly forty years in the area and this left very little time to do the research needed for the book. I asked for a few days to think about it.

I did not need a few days. I knew before I left the house that I wanted to write the book, but I thought it might look better if I made it look like a considered decision. I also needed to sleep on it and to plan in my mind how such a book would evolve.

Two things happened in my favour. One was that the house was not selling. It was very frustrating because although we had a very enjoyable and active social life in Bristol we wanted to move north to enjoy our children and grandchildren. The second thing was that the more I thought about it the more the story just seemed to fall into place. I had accumulated enough knowledge about Bristol to know where to find all the published information on St Mary Redcliffe. We made a visit to the Bristol Record Office and there we discovered many useful unpublished records but most valuable of all were the parish magazines going back to Victorian times. These magazines, together with the publications of the Canynges Society, enabled me to discover anecdotes from the nineteenth and twentieth centuries and to bring the history right up to the present time.

As well as John and Sue Pickard I want to acknowledge my wife Dilys, Roger Feneley, John Pickard for photography and all the parishioners especially those who have contributed to the parish magazine.

Peter Aughton, April 2008

An imaginary view of the nave, looking east towards the Hogarth altarpiece and stripped of monuments and pews in order to reveal the architectural detail; plate VIII from John Britton's pioneering *Historical and architectural essay relating to Redcliffe Church*, published in 1813.

CHAPTER ONE

Brig Stow

Where the northern boundary of Alfred the Great's Wessex met the southern boundary of the ancient kingdom of Mercia there ran a swiftly flowing river that drained the lands to the east. The Avon may have been a lesser river than the Severn or the Thames but on its way to the sea it carved out a great limestone gorge 200 feet in depth, a chasm as deep and spectacular as any in the whole of England. The river could be forded at the deepest and narrowest part of the gorge, at the point where the rocks made a hard bottom, but the ford was only a few miles from the sea and the tidal waters came in rapidly with great force to trap the unwary men and cattle who tried to cross without local knowledge. Many had lost their lives trying to cross the Avon, but as the first millennium drew to a close a bridge was built of sturdy Saxon timberwork to join together the kingdoms of Wessex and Mercia.

At this time trading posts were long established both north and south of the bridge. The bulk of the trade was that of the farmers' weekly markets of the inland shires. There were fruits and vegetables, poultry and livestock for sale. There was cloth and simple clothing for the farm labourer. There were tools of iron and implements of husbandry. The river was navigable to small craft for many miles to the inland and it brought traders from the Roman settlement at Aquae Sulis and other towns to the east. Even more important was the fact that the river was also navigable to the estuary of the river Severn, giving easy access to the Welsh coast and also to the long meandering thread of the Severn running deep into the country to the north. Most important of all, the river Avon gave access to the sea which girdled the great world beyond. From the earliest times items of scarcity and exotic foreign manufacture were exchanged at the bridge place. It rapidly grew to such a busy trading centre that by the time of Ethelred the Unready coins were being minted on or near the bridge. A Saxon town came into being. It became known as the Brig Stow meaning the town of the bridge. It soon developed houses, taverns and churches.

The town that grew at the bridge was close to the confluence of two rivers and the lesser river, called the Frome, joined the Avon at the marshy land just downstream from the bridge. It was obvious that the land between the Avon and the Frome was the

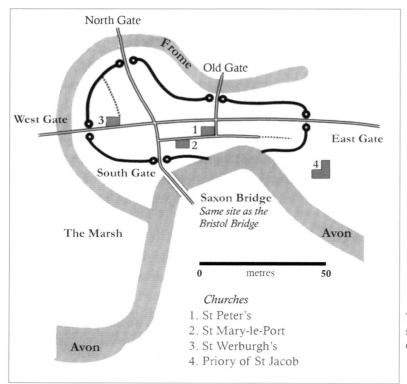

The extent of Saxon Bristol showing the gates and four churches.

Churches
1. St Peter's
2. St Mary-le-Port
3. St Werburgh's
4. Priory of St Jacob

best place to build a fortified town, the Frome was easily bridged but it still provided a natural defence against invasion from the north. The existence of the Frome was the reason why Brig Stow was centred on the north of the river rather than on the south. When it came to repelling unwanted visitors only the eastern side of the town needed extra fortification. The Saxon town became a walled town. By the time of the Norman conquest there were three churches: St Peter's, St Mary-le-Port and St Werburgh's. There was also a priory just outside the walls, dedicated to St Jacob.[1]

Robert Fitzharding was the founder of the Abbey of St Augustine and he was, therefore, partly responsible for the beautiful chapter house which, with its interlaced arcading and ornate vaulting ribs became his greatest memorial and eventually part of Bristol Cathedral. The Norman Conquest of 1066 seemed at first to be a severe setback to the development of Anglo-Saxon England, but the Normans were great organisers and builders and it was not long before Brig Stow began to prosper and expand again. The town's defences were strengthened by building a more substantial wall and by a castle, a great fortified keep to protect the east of the town against invasion.

Thus, by the beginning of the twelfth century, the trade and population of the area merchandise from lands near and far'.[3] Some of the Bristol merchants found the south bank was a good place to trade, the deeper waters making the river more navigable when the tide was low. Many of the traders from the south could purchase their wares at the quayside and save the extra time and hassle of crossing the bridge into Bristol. The population of the south bank of the Avon began to grow rapidly in the twelfth century. It was found necessary to have a new place of worship and early in the century the lords of Bedminster decided to build a new chapel on a hillock near the bend in the river. The chapel seems to have been crown property for a deed survives from the year 1115 in which the king gives 'the chapel of Redclive' to the diocese of Salisbury. The church must have been a chapel of ease to the Norman church of St John's Bedminster.

This is the earliest recorded reference to a church at Redcliffe.

1. Aughton Chapter 1

2. Little Chapter 2

3. K R Potter (ed): *Gesta Stephani Oxford Medieval Texts* (1976) pp 56-59

CHAPTER TWO

Early English

The deed from 1115 creates more problems than it solves. It implies that a church already existed at that time on the site at Redcliffe. If this was the case then nothing at all survives to tell us anything about it, yet we know that a very large and fine church, in the Early English style, was constructed on the site a few decades later from the middle of the twelfth century. A probable explanation is that the church of 1115 was very small and was completely obliterated by the major re-buildings that followed over the next three centuries. Fragments of Norman zig-zag mouldings have been found but the records of the time are silent. It is reasonable to assume that it was named after St Mary but even this detail cannot be confirmed. All we can say with some confidence is that by the second half of the century construction had begun on a new church at Redcliffe; it could have been built on a nearby site or it could have been an upgrading of the existing chapel on the same site. The ground plans were laid out and work on the foundations began.

Church architecture was always evolving to create newer, lighter, more elegant and flamboyant forms. The Norman architecture superseded the cruder techniques of the Saxons. A hundred years after the Norman Conquest the heavy rounded arches of the Normans were out of fashion. The pointed arch could carry more weight with less stone and this was the basis of the new Early English architecture that became the fashion of the time. Windows were built with stone tracery. Doorways were pointed and had elaborate decorations. Roofs could be vaulted in stone. Columns of stone were clustered together with complex groupings of the columns. Decorative carvings of leaves, flowers, faces and even animals appeared on bases and capitals.

From about 1140 the area around Redcliffe Hill became a building site. Lumbering oxcarts arrived bringing the newly cut stone from the Mendip quarries at Dundry, Chew and beyond. The stone was stored in the mason's yard where rough blocks were worked into shape by the labourers and the master's apprentices. As the walls began to grow the heavy medieval scaffolding appeared – a sight that was to obscure the view of the church for a long time to come.

Thus, the church which began to rise on Redcliffe Hill was Early English in style.

The south wall seemed to be in keeping with the new style, but there were still Romanesque rounded arches on the north side of the nave, a possible relict of the church mentioned in 1115. This fine new church was of grand proportions, with a nave consisting of six or seven bays. The nave had aisles to both north and south. There were no transepts but there was a very elaborate north porch decorated with blue columns very like Purbeck marble but actually a local substitute called blue lias. The door from the porch to the church had a gothic arch with a flamboyant pattern of five plus seven plus five rolls. It was significant that the grand main entrance to the church was on the same side as the river where most wealthy parishioners lived.

During this first phase of construction Lord

For centuries the people of Redcliffe drew their water from the pipe supply. This shows the old outlet, beneath the stone balustrades to the west of the church.

The inner north porch dates from about 1185 and it was the main entrance to the church for 100 years, until the outer porch was built.

Robert de Berkeley: the oldest known benefactor of the church. It was he who gave a water supply to Redcliffe in 1190. His wife Juliana gave land for the pipe – the only fresh water supply in Redcliffe for 500 years.

Robert de Berkeley gave the church a water conduit and a well called the Ruge Well which is traditionally dated from the year 1190. The conduit carried water from the Knowle area and the well, situated at the west end of the church, became the main supply of fresh water for Redcliffe. It was his wife Juliana who gave the land for the pipe to be laid from the spring to Redcliffe and for 500 years it was the only supply of fresh water. It is not known when the earliest pipe walk took place but it became a tradition for parishioners to walk along the route of the pipe every year to ensure that the water supply was properly maintained. The well head was a meeting place where women and children came to draw water. News and gossip was exchanged and it helped the church to become part of the community.

The Ruge Well also supplied water to St John's Hospital which was only a short distance from the church near the banks of the Avon. The hospital was founded in 1215 by Robert de Berkeley and in 1219 there is mention of a master and several brethren to tend to the sick and also to provide accommodation for travellers. St John's was seemingly a hospice as well as a hospital. Both brothers and sisters are mentioned in the deeds of the hospital and the implication is that both sexes were catered for. The hospital was allowed to lay an extra pipe from the Ruge Well to carry its own water

The corbels are survivals from the Early English church. They are carvings representing townsmen of Bristol, struggling to hold up a great weight of stone. The corbels were also used as capitals at the top of a column, so that instead of a statue they might support part of the church structure.

The water supply as it was in 1932: a new exit with Latin inscriptions commemorating Robert de Berkeley.

supply. The pipe extension was built early in the thirteenth century, at the time of King John and there are records in later years of workmen who were allowed access to the chapel yard of St Mary's to repair the pipe. An early thirteenth-century seal of the hospital of St John survives depicting the baptism of Jesus and the wording 'Sigill Hospital Sci Johis Baptiste de Radeclivia'. St John's Hospital is mentioned again in 1286 when the master, Stephen, illegally built a gate across the public road. He was fined twenty shillings and ordered to take it down again.

The years became decades and the decades became generations. The church building progressed slowly. By the end of the century men whose grandfathers had worked on the new church were working on it themselves. The thirteenth century arrived and still the work was in progress. There is a mention of a bell tower as early as 1208 but no details are given. This was either a temporary structure to enable the bells to be rung or possibly a small detached tower, a miniature campanile as was the fashion in Italy. The foundations for the great tower were laid in about 1240 on the north-west corner of the church and they were as much as five feet thick in places. The tower was designed from the outset to rise to a great height and to carry a great weight of stone. To the south west a small detached chapel was built in the same Early English style as the church, and dedicated to the Holy Spirit. Small services could be held in the chapel without the distractions of the major building works.

As the middle of the thirteenth century approached, the north wall had reached its full height and the south wall was nearing completion. The nave was high, possibly rising to fifty feet, and it was to be vaulted in stone. The roof arches and the niches for the statues were supported by medieval corbels: great carved stone brackets with ugly figures of men or mythical stone animals. Lions' faces appeared, beasts with bats' ears and cloven hooves, some of the animals partly clothed and others with human heads. One very beautiful feature of the church was the singer's galleries located in the main walls. This was a feature found in the cathedrals of Wells, Lichfield and Salisbury. The

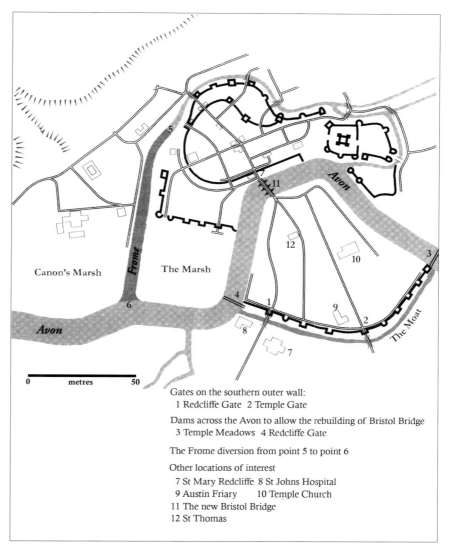

Gates on the southern outer wall:
  1 Redcliffe Gate 2 Temple Gate

Dams across the Avon to allow the rebuilding of Bristol Bridge
  3 Temple Meadows 4 Redcliffe Gate

The Frome diversion from point 5 to point 6

Other locations of interest
  7 St Mary Redcliffe 8 St Johns Hospital
  9 Austin Friary   10 Temple Church
  11 The new Bristol Bridge
  12 St Thomas

Bristol in 1250.

galleries were openings where, during the chants, a singer would stand and the notes of a pure solo voice would ring out through the church as though the singing was coming from heaven above.

In the century since the foundation of the church there had been major changes in Brig Stow. The place was usually called by the name Bristow although, because the local population had problems pronouncing the 'w', this eventually became Bristol. The name hovered between these two spellings for another century or more before reaching its final form. Sometimes the place was referred to as Brightstow or Bright Bow and this seems to have been the name used by residents south of the river. The bridge is sometimes called 'Brightstowe Bridge'. Even as late as Elizabethan times

(1581) there appears a plan of 'Brightstowe' by Hofnagle which shows the whole of Bristol. Earlier references imply that Brightstowe may have been the area south of the river, between the bridge and Bedminster.

In about 1189, towards the last year of the reign of Henry II, Bristol had received its first charter giving certain trading rights and privileges. The housing development and the trade of the port of Bristol obviously expanded as rapidly as did the ecclesiastical life even though it was less well documented. Bristol had become a thriving mercantile town with a population advancing from over a thousand towards two thousand by the year 1200. The centre of the Norman town was at the crossroads where Corn Street and Wynch Street met Broad Street and High Street, the latter being the route to the timber bridge across the Avon.

In the thirteenth century merchants on the Gloucestershire bank sought for some means of expanding and improving their wharf space as the river traffic became progressively more and more chaotic. If Bristol was to expand its maritime trade a radical improvement in shipping facilities was needed. It was not only the wharf space which was inadequate, the old Saxon bridge could not cope with the amount of traffic crossing it. The town had already outgrown its Norman defensive walls and the prosperous expanding suburbs on the Somerset banks had no protection against invasion from the south.

Three ambitious new building schemes were forwarded and all three were approved. One was to build a new set of city walls to include part of the Somerset side of the river with extensions to the wall on the Gloucestershire side as well. A second scheme was to replace the overworked wooden bridge over the Avon with a new stone bridge of four arches. The third and most ambitious scheme was to divert the river Frome to provide extra wharf space near the centre of the town. There were many parallels with the City of London. In London, as with Bristol, the centre had developed on the north bank of the river leaving the south bank rather isolated. London Bridge was built about fifty years before the new Bristol Bridge and the river Thames had been diverted to allow the construction of the bridge. London Bridge was nineteen arches long, Bristol only four, but Bristolians felt that whatever the Londoners could achieve they could achieve as well.

A new channel was cut from a point on the Avon, above the Saxon bridge at the Temple meadows, to a point at Redcliffe Back. Then the whole river was dammed and

The vaulting of the outer north porch dates from about 1290 and is designed to span the hexagonal shape of the porch.

diverted to flow through the new channel. The diverted river flowed right past the northern entrance to the church of St Mary Redcliffe. The waterway was later retained and used as a moat for the new southern city wall. Redcliffe Parish was cut in two, for part of it lay inside the walls whilst the church and the southern half lay outside.

A second dam was built just downstream from the Bristol Bridge so that, with the river diverted, the townsfolk of Bristol gazed down on a dry riverbed where their timber bridge had stood. The foundations for the new town bridge, to be built of stone, were under construction. In the bed of the Avon three central piers were built with a pier on each bank to give four stone arches supporting a road wide enough for houses and shops. When it was completed Bristol Bridge became a much sought-after place to live, rentals were amongst the highest in the town – one of the main reasons for its popularity was probably the sanitary arrangements which were far more effective than anything in the heart of town!

The plan for the diversion of the river Frome was even more ambitious. A trench was to be built 750 yards long – deep and wide enough to take ocean-going craft – and the Frome would be diverted from its course around the west wall of Bristol into this new channel. The new watercourse would provide as much mooring space as the Avon and it would double the number of ships that the port could service at any one time. The Redcliffe merchants, however, felt that they would not benefit from the new facilities and when they discovered that they were expected to shoulder part of the cost they became very much opposed to the scheme. The Gloucestershire merchants were determined to have their way. They claimed that the works were of benefit to the whole town, and managed to obtain royal assent. In 1239 the work was underway and in the following year Henry III wrote personally to the men of Redcliffe:

> …Whereas our beloved burgesses of Bristol for the common good for the whole town of Bristol as of your suburb have begun a certain trench in the Marsh of St Augustine that ships coming to our port of Bristol may be able to enter or leave more freely and without impediment; which trench they will indeed be unable to perfect without great costs. We command you that, wheras from the betterment of the same port not only to the burgesses themselves but also to you, who are partakers of the same liberties which our aforesaid burgesses have in the town aforesaid and in scot and lot you are fellows with them, no little advantage ought to accrue. Moreover it may be very useful and fruitful for you for the work of the trench aforesaid to be perfected successfully according as it concerns you together with our aforesaid burgesses, to whom as sharers in the liberties aforesaid you shall give like efficacious aid as they themselves do, lest the aforesaid work, which we regard as our own, through your defection should receive delay.[1]

In the year 1210 King John had imposed a tax which was called his 'Special Aid', and Redcliffe was required to pay a thousand marks, the same as the sum paid by Bristol proper and the implication is that in this century Redcliffe was considered to be as wealthy as the rest of Bristol put together.

The Redcliffe men were therefore forced to pay their share of the cost of the new trench, but there were some consolations. Their legal pleas were henceforth allowed to be heard in Bristol and this saved them the long journey to the Somerset court at Ilchester – it was a forerunner of the application in the next century to make Bristol into a self-governing unit. The episode of the new mooring space created a rivalry between the Gloucestershire and Somerset factions and this may well be one of the reasons why the Redcliffe men were determined to build a larger and finer church than any of their rivals north of the river.

As the new trench progressed there were similar scenes of activity in the south and the west of the town. Wooden scaffolding was erected in the Redcliffe area, the masons' hammers and chisels rang out day after day as the new walls took shape, complete with rounded towers at intervals and new fortified gateways for the roads leading out of town to the south. In the north, where the great new trench was being excavated to accommodate the seagoing traffic of maritime Bristol, even more impressive works were underway. Primitive cranes with wooden treadmills were used for lifting the heavy stones to build the masonry quay on the Bristol bank, but the excavation of the great trench was achieved entirely by man and beast. The ground was marshy and the work was excruciatingly wet and muddy. In the deep channel well below ground level hundreds of labourers scraped at the earth, shifting the mud and muck by barrow load up timber-lined ramps to the surface. Other workers hauled with ropes, rollers and levers to bring the cut stone from the local quarries to build the quay wall. It is difficult to find harbour works on this scale in the Middle Ages with which to compare the new quay. The cost was five thousand pounds, an enormous sum of money comparable to that of the great castles and cathedrals, but the nature of the work was quite different: it was a work of man rather than a work of God, and it was much more in keeping with the canal and railway ages which lay far in the future.

By 1247 the great new trench was completed, the dam was broken and the waters of the Frome gushed into the new channel. It was a great day for Bristol when the first wooden vessels moored against the new quay. The new man-made harbour served the port for centuries to come and it was considered one of the greatest civil engineering works of the Middle Ages.

The new quay was a great success and Bristol continued to grow at a rapid rate. The rivalry continued between the north and south banks of the Avon. It was true that the south bank benefited from the increased trade in the north but by the end of the thirteenth century there were many more people living on the Gloucestershire bank than on the Somerset bank. Bristol north of the Avon, however, had many small parishes. There were fourteen of them cramped inside the city walls to the north of the bridge but to the south there were only three parishes. These three were St Thomas, Temple and St Mary Redcliffe. Consequently these parishes, and St Mary Redcliffe in particular, became considerably wealthier than any of their northern rivals.

In the early 1300s the mayor and burgesses of Bristol held a court in Redcliffe Street

William James Muller *North porch*, 1832, pencil, Bristol Museums and Art Gallery (M3152)
No drawing better illustrates the appalling state of dilapidation of the decorative stonework on the north porch, all of which was soon to be completely recarved.

where there was a prison to confine any offenders. The weekly market in Redcliffe Street was well established at this time but some in Bristol wanted to put a stop to it and to abolish all distinctions between the north and south portions of the town. They wanted justice to be dealt out north of the river. The Lords of Berkeley still held the land at Bedminster and Redcliffe however and it was technically outside Gloucestershire and was part of Somerset. They won their case and continued to hold their court at Redcliffe, pleadings were heard and criminals were sentenced to prison or to the pillory. It was not until 1373 that Bristol received its most important charter, making it a self-governing unit and a county in its own right.[2]

The Early English church at Redcliffe was without doubt a church of great style and beauty, but missing from our description are the names of the people connected with the early church. There is mention of repairs to the church in 1207, 1229 and 1230. In 1232 the name of Helen Wedmore appears as a benefactor. In 1246 appears David, Archbishop of Cashel, followed in 1278 by Robert the Bishop of Bath and Wells and in 1287 by Peter Quivil the Bishop of Exeter. At this time the nave of the new church was near to completion. The roof was vaulted in stone, the nave had a north and south aisle and a clerestory. The walls were decorated with medieval paintings showing scenes from the gospels, a common ecclesiastical feature in these early centuries. The tower was still under construction and it was not completed until a few decades later, but towards the middle of the thirteenth century the scaffolding was removed from the nave and the parishioners could enjoy their new church to the full.

At the end of the century it was decided to build an outer porch onto the existing inner porch. The new porch was of a very grand and unique design that has given historians great problems with the dating. Dates from 1290 to 1330 have been suggested. The porch was hexagonal in plan, a unique design in English church architecture. It was very tall with a lantern-shaped space high above the door level, illuminated by high windows with a walkway round them. Most fascinating of all was the unique external décor around the door. Here was a very intricate Islamic design that must have been inspired by the growing trade between Bristol and the exotic east. Winged angels appear in attitudes of prayer, surrounded by carved leaves and foliage, strange winged beasts stare down and mythical birds perch on the corners. Outside there were many niches with statues of the kings of England. Inside the porch was a church in miniature, the hexagonal plane rose to a stone-vaulted roof with elaborate bosses, very high with the beautiful windows giving light like a lantern from high above. The outer door was built with a unique, many pointed, design. Access to the church was through the older inner porch, making the two porches a very elaborate entrance to the main body of the church.

During the time the outer porch was built the spire continued to grow, soaring slowly higher and higher towards the heavens. It owed much of its inspiration to Salisbury and it was completed in about 1320 at the astonishing height of 285 feet. Salisbury of course, was much higher at 404 feet, but Salisbury was a great cathedral. St Mary Redcliffe, strictly speaking, was only a chapel of ease to Bedminster Parish Church.

Nobody could wish for a more beautiful or attractive church than the Early English church of Redcliffe. Could they?

1. N Dermott Harding (ed): *Bristol Charters 1155-1373*, Bristol Record Society 1, 1930 p19

2. Little, Chapter 4

CHAPTER THREE

Perpendicular and Decorated

Why, when a century and a half had been spent in building a fine church at Redcliffe, did the powers that be want to rebuild their beautiful church? The most likely explanation is that Bristol was prospering and the wealthy merchants therefore had more to spend on public works and churches. They had money to improve Redcliffe Church. The existing style of the architecture, said the modernists, was that of the last century. The new Perpendicular style was far grander and more impressive. It was true that the nave of the Early English church was vaulted in stone and the roof was a respectable height, but the nave was no more than a simple rectangle when a cruciform plan with transepts to north and south would be far more impressive.

The Early English church at Redcliffe had become available as a place of worship in the thirteenth century but building still continued almost unbroken from that time. The outer porch, as we have seen, was constructed towards the end of the century but it may not have been completed until about 1320. Over the same period, in the northwest corner of the church, the tower was still under construction and at the turn of the century, as soon as it was completed, the spire was built on top of it. The south porch was under construction at much the same time and the opportunity was taken to reconstruct the wall of the south aisle in the new style. There may have been a short break, a single decade around the 1320s, when the building stopped. Then in about 1330 the decision was taken to completely rebuild the church in the latest style with a grand cruciform plan. The building started all over again.

The reconstruction of the south wall had probably been achieved by rebuilding the wall one bay at a time without dismantling the whole wall or, more significantly, without having to remove the vaulted stone roof. No building work could be done on the Sabbath or the other important Christian festivals but the gaps in the wall, the scaffolds, and the windows open to the wintry elements were a major impediment to the services. The Chapel of the Holy Spirit could be used for funerals and small services but it was far too small to hold the whole congregation.

Thus, as the grand plan for the new church was laid out, St Mary Redcliffe became a building site all over again. To cause minimum interruption it seems likely that the east end of the new church and the north and south transepts were the next phase of construction, after rebuilding the south wall. This would not interfere directly with the services held in the nave of the old church. The chancel and the chancel aisles were constructed, as was the Lady Chapel except for the final bay at the eastern end which was built later and is dated at about 1400. When the new part of the church was eventually completed, roofed and vaulted, the congregation could use the two new transepts for their church whilst the old church was rebuilt and re-vaulted to match the same style as the new.

For generations there had hardly been a year when there was no building going on.

Outside the church and above the west door are six of the saints, seated and holding their staffs of office.

But this is what seems so remarkable when we look back 700 years. The people of the time did not see it in the same way. They had always known it thus. They remembered the building in their youth. Their parents and grandparents remembered the building when they, in turn, were young. The Early English church had been in use for over a hundred years and by the time it had been rebuilt there was nobody in the whole of Bristol old enough to remember the time before it existed.

The exterior of the new church showed an upper and a lower row of tall windows with delicate tracery, a uniform design on north and south transepts, nave and choir with aisles both north and south. On the outside the onlooker saw the flying buttresses

Opposite: There are over a thousand roof bosses in St Mary Redcliffe. *Above, clockwise from top left*: a vaulting pattern of the high vault in the north transept; sun god; the Berkeley arms and a maze – probably unique to a boss and recreated in a local park.

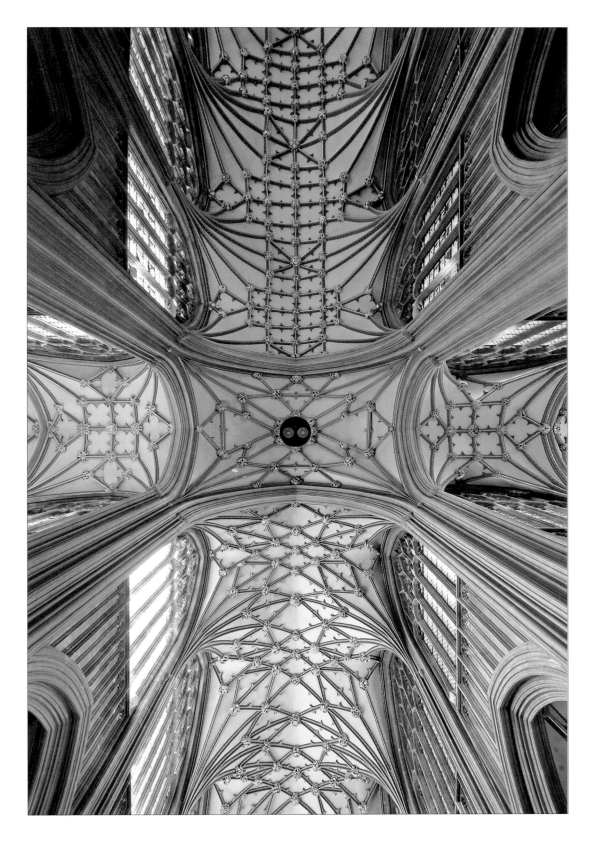

holding the lateral thrust of the higher walls of the clerestory and above every buttress was mounted a gothic pinnacle. The interior of the church was a stone forest of vertical perpendicular columns, the play of light through the windows making beautiful patterns on walls and floor. High above was the vaulted roof with many variations on the patterns of the vaulting, depending on the problems they were designed to solve. The roof was supported by the bosses, individually shaped keystones which were a necessary part of the construction but which provided an ideal vehicle for the mason to show off his art. There were over a thousand roof bosses with designs including the Trinity, the Annunciation, the Coronation of the Virgin and many more.

In the north transept one boss shows a mermaid with a comb in one hand and a glass in the other. The south aisle has several grotesque heads, two bosses have shafts issuing from their mouths, and one seems to be a grinning fish composed of leaves. The high central nave has the most elaborate bosses, including the crucifixion and a marvellous depiction of the Virgin and Child. In the other bays the masons seem to have been given a free licence to use their art; there are monkeys, lions, dragons, a weasel chasing a rabbit and a monstrous beaked fish swallowing another beast with bat's wings. In the fourth bay of the north aisle is the maze boss, a unique circular design which is perhaps the most famous of them all. Martin Lee has created a volume listing all the bosses.[1]

For many years it was assumed that the Canynges family were the main benefactors in the building of St Mary Redcliffe. Certainly the Canynges must have made some contribution, but their involvement has been greatly exaggerated. It is not possible to publish a tidy list of benefactors with the amounts contributed by each one, but in the new church of the fourteenth century appear the heraldic arms of four powerful families carved in stone on the aisle-vault bosses at the north-west crossing. They include the Berkeleys, who always had an historical interest in the church as lords of the ancient Bedminster Manor, plus the families of Beauchamp, Stafford and Montacute. These four families were probably the main contributors to the building of the new church. In the fourteenth century we can also, at long last, confidently give the names of the vicars. They were Henry de Aston from 1320, John Hamond from 1322, John Doudswell for a few months in 1329 followed by Robert de Alne who replaced him later in the same year. In 1344 Robert de Alne was followed by Richard de Chippenham for what turned out to be a short incumbency of only a few years.

The time has come to take a short break from the rebuilding of the church so that we can study the times. The most horrific and shattering event of the fourteenth century was the spread of the terrible bubonic plague which is remembered as the Black Death. It arrived in England from the continent in 1348 and raged through the country unchecked throughout that year and also in the following year. Records are seldom preserved for the ordinary people who died, but one way to collect statistics is from the records of the clergy. It is significant that John Blonkes became the vicar of St Mary Redcliffe in 1350. This does not prove that Richard de Chippenham died from the bubonic plague which broke out in 1348, but when we allow the time taken to find a replacement for him when the whole administrative structure of the country was in chaos, we must consider the Black Death as the most likely cause of his decease.

The population of England was reduced by about a third, in some places by as much as a half. When the plague at last died out there was a great deal of sorting out to be done. Money was not a real problem, many had inherited through the untimely deaths of their parents and some wanted to put money into the rebuilding of the church. The problem was that it was almost impossible to find labour and skilled men such as stone masons could charge very high prices for their work.

Now consider. The bulk of the church of St Mary Redcliffe seems to have been constructed in the period 1350 to 1375. This includes the walls of both the north and south transepts, the choir and sanctuary, the Lady Chapel and three bays of the north aisle. About two thirds of the whole wall structure, not to mention the roofing and the floor-work, seems to have been constructed in this 25-year period and at a time when there had never been such a shortage of skilled workers and labourers in England.

The Black Death did not respect class or money. Many of the wealthy could have left large sums towards the completion of the church. It is possible to identify some of these benefactors but even if we can decide who paid for it all we cannot solve the problem of where they found the labour, especially when we consider that many of the other Bristol churches were also rebuilding at this time. What we do know is that by about 1375 the beautiful gothic church was completed. It was the church that we know and see today with its pinnacles and flying buttresses, its soaring columns, its beautiful windows with stone tracery and its vaulted stone roof with over a thousand roof bosses. Most of the histories say that it is the third church on the site, the first being the Norman church mentioned in 1115 and the second being the Early English church as it appeared in the decades before 1300. We know so little of the Norman

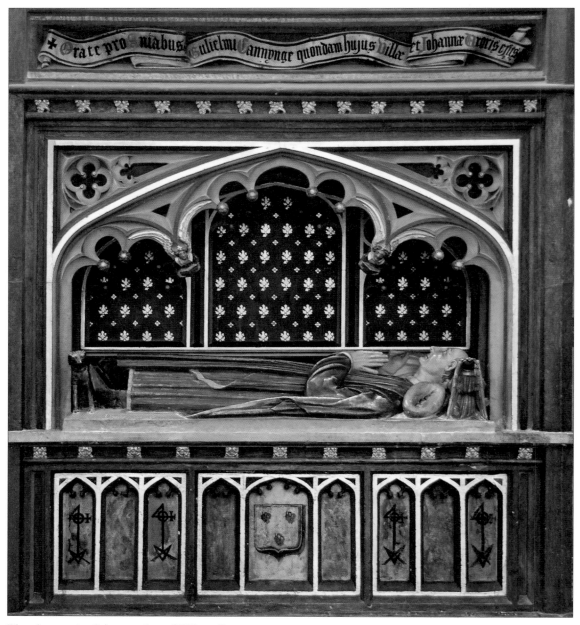

The altar tomb of the merchant William Canynges.

church that we cannot envisage what it was like. The nave of the Early English church was completed by 1300 but the spire was still under construction until 1320. Thus, from the 1100s right through to about 1375, there was hardly a pause in the building process. For an era of more than 200 years there was nothing but building.

But the new church must have satisfied even the most particular of the Redcliffe

The south porch does not get the attention of the north porch but it is a fine feature of the church. It was built in about 1320 and predates the main structure of the church by about 40 years.

congregation. On the approach to Bristol from the south, and the west and the east, the beautiful church on the hill with its soaring spire, its perpendicular windows and its magnificent flying buttresses was the most prominent feature on the skyline. Approaching over the hills from the north, as the buildings of Bristol appeared in front and below the traveller, the spire of St Mary's stood out behind the town with its Gothic pinnacles reaching towards heaven in its awesome beauty.

1. Martin Lee: *The Boss Walk* (1999)

CHAPTER FOUR

New Found Land

Walking up and down the churchyard of St Mary Redcliffe was an eccentric, elderly man. He counted his paces as he walked. Sometimes he would change his walking pattern and instead of striding out he would carefully put heel to toe for a short distance. He was counting, always counting. When he found an item of interest he would stop and stare at it. Then he produced a piece of parchment and scribbled down a few notes.

Who was this man who showed such an interest in the church? He had been born in Bristol about 65 years earlier but as a youth had left his birthplace to go to college at Oxford. He had family in Bristol, his sister Joan lived in Redcliffe Street and she was the widow of merchant John Jay, an active member of the congregation. The man's name was William Worcestre, and his appearance was deceptive, he was a man far ahead of his times. He had taken it upon himself to measure the whole of Bristol, the roads, the churches, the bridges, the gates and the walls, and all the main buildings. He was very open about his survey and he would gossip to anybody he could find to get his information. He chatted to John Norton, the master mason of Redcliffe church. He discovered that the church spire, which Worcestre had known in his youth at its soaring height of nearly 300 feet, had been 'Thrown down by chance in a storm of lightening'. He estimated that the top of the truncated spire which remained was a mere 200 feet above the ground. This second-hand account from John Norton seems to be the only surviving record of what was a terrible catastrophe. If lives were lost when the spire fell then the dead were not recorded. If the church was seriously damaged by the fall then there is little evidence to show. The lack of damage to the nave and north porch implies that the fall was probably to the west and away from the main body of the church.

The date of 1445 or 1446 is frequently quoted for the fall of the spire and William Worcestre is given as the authority for this date. In the whole of Worcestre's notes on Bristol, however, he nowhere records an actual date for the catastrophe. When William Worcestre left Bristol as a youth in about 1430 the spire was still standing. When he returned in 1468 the spire had fallen some years before. The strange thing is that

The Mede brass dates from about 1475. The inscription reads '... the aforementioned Thomas Mede and three times Mayor of this town of Bristol who died 20... day of December 1475 on whose soul may the Lord have mercy: amen.'

William Worcestre must have known almost exactly when the catastrophe occurred. He retained contact with his family all the time he was away, his sister worshipped at St Mary's and she must have told him of the fall of the spire. He also had a son who may well have lived in Bristol. It is fortunate that *Adam s Chronicle of Bristol* mentions the fall of the steeple. In 1445 the chronicle says that 'This year Redclife steeple in Bristoll was thrown down by a thunderclap, which did much harm also in other places'. It is a strange coincidence that there is little documentation covering the period in question, there are no surviving church records from that time and we have very little knowledge of the church from the first half of the fifteenth century. There is an intriguing theory about this gap in the records, but the story belongs to a later century and will be withheld for the time being.

Amongst the few names from the early fifteenth century are those of Richard Foster,

The tomb of Thomas Mede.

a burgess, who in 1450 left 13s 4d to the repair of the church fabric. In 1460 Maurice White left 6s 8d to the same cause. These are isolated records but the earliest of the church brasses date from this period and they give a little more information. The earliest brass, set in a stone of Purbeck marble, is that of Sir John Juyn who died in 1439. He was the recorder of Bristol. He is shown standing with hands clasped in prayer wearing a close cap and a fur-lined mantle. In the north choir ambulatory is a double tomb of Thomas Mede and his wife and also his brother Philip Mede who died in 1475. There is a beautiful brass of Philip in an attitude of prayer with his two wives; a great deal of detail is shown in the dress and even the facial expressions. The inscription is unfortunately missing but there are scrolls on the brass itself which read, after translation from the Latin, 'Holy Trinity God pity us' and 'God, the Father of Heaven, pity us.' Later brasses include that of John Jay (died 1480) and Johanna (or Joan) his wife and a very fine brass to John and Johanna Brook, dating from 1522 but relating to the fifteenth-century family connection with Richard Ameryk.

William Worcestre never completed his survey. There were many places in his notes where he left a blank space because he did not know the correct figure to enter. His notes are scrappy and repetitive, they are full of errors and he never had time to put them into order before he died in 1485. What remains of his findings, however, is a remarkable and unique survey of a medieval city. In one extract we can calculate how long his stride was, for it is measured in both steps and yards.

> In the eastern road from Redcliffe Church [by] the Lady chapel is a long wall towards Pylle Hill well, going to St Anne's. The said wall measures 50 yards or 70 steps in length (The number of yards was counted by my son) to the beginning of the wall next to the east side of the churchyard of the said church.[1]

This is the only passage in Worcestre's itinerary which mentions his son. Since the father was 65 we may assume that the son was not a boy at the time but a grown man. The father gives us other details of the church as he picked his way heel to toe around the bell tower:

> The length of the bell-tower upon the newly-built vault measures 24 feet from east to west, and 22 feet from north to south. Also, of the square foundation of the construction of Redcliffe spire, which is of eight panels: the first course of the spire, upon the squared base, consists of a two-foot thickness of stones, from two stones cemented together, because it is hard to obtain a single stone of such thickness. And so it continues, diminishing up to a certain height; and there are four corbels of stone, at each of the four corners, to hold together the spire; which same spire now stands more than 100 feet.[2]

He estimated the length of the church at 63 yards plus another 13 yards for the Lady Chapel at the east end.

He took a great interest in the Canynges family. He saw the elaborate memorial to William Canynges the younger and gives us some information about him. Canynges was a very wealthy shipping merchant. He was five times mayor of Bristol and in his later years, after the death of his wife, he had taken holy orders and he became involved with the college at Westbury-on-Trym.[3] He spent much of his fortune on Westbury College and by the time of his death in 1474 he had become Dean of the College.

A memorial board gives valuable information about the life of William Canynges. It includes the names of ten ships with their burthens, including the *Mary Redcliffe* of 500 tuns.

Canynges was a benefactor of St Mary Redcliffe, he founded two chantries and his prominent memorial in the church testifies to his support, but the popular theory that he was mainly responsible for the whole rebuilding of the church has been shown to be a gross exaggeration. In fact the church was completed long before he was born.[4]

Worcestre mentions a college of chaplains with a hall or residence. Forty steps across Redcliffe Hill were the workshops of the stonemasons 'for the construction of Redcliffe Church'. The construction was long finished but there was obviously plenty of maintenance required and he has already told us about the master mason John Norton. He studied the effigy of William Canynges the younger in the south transept and he noted the memorial to William Coke, Canynges' cook, with its colander and a knife. He tells us that William Canynges employed 900 men at work on his ships. He gives a list of the ships owned by Canynges, taken from the plaque near the tomb. One of them is named after the church at Redcliffe and it is a moving thought to imagine the *Mary Redcliffe* riding the heavy swell and the storms of the Atlantic Ocean:

> The Mary Canynges, of 400 tons
>
> The Mary Redcliffe of 500 tons weight
>
> The Mary and John of 900 tons weight, cost him 4,000 marks in all

The Galliot, a ship of 50 tons weight

The Catherine, of 140 tons weight

The Marybat, of 220 tons weight

The Margaret of Tynly, of 200 tons weight

The Little Nicholas, of 140 tons weight

The Katherine of Boston, of 220 tons weight

The … , a ship lost off Iceland, weight of about 160 tons[5]

The story of the ship lost off Iceland is intriguing. Bristol merchants traded regularly as far out into the Atlantic as Iceland and sometimes they brought back reports of land sightings far to the west. At the time of William Worcestre's visit in 1480 his sister Joan was waiting for news of John Jay the younger, whom we think was a half-brother of John Jay, her late husband. Jay had sailed on a voyage of exploration beyond the west of Ireland in search of the Island of Brasil which was reputed to lie somewhere in that direction. In September came news that the ship was safe in Ireland but no new discoveries had been made on the voyage. John Jay's ship of eighty tons sailed from Bristol on 15 July 1480 and returned in September. We are given a few particulars of the voyage including the name of the ship's master:

On the south side of the chancel beyond the choir stalls is the brass of John Jay and his wife Joan. Joan was the sister of William Worcestre, the Bristol topographer who features in the text. Note their six sons and eight daughters beneath.

Opposite: A modern wooden carving by Roy Bishop of the voyage of the *Matthew* in 1497 and the 500th anniversary voyage of the replica ship.

… Lloyde was the ship's master, the most knowledgeable mariner in all England. And news came to Bristol on Monday, the 18th day of September that the said ship had sailed the sea for about 9 months [an error for 9 weeks], not finding the islands, but was driven back by storms at sea to the port of… in Ireland, for refitting the ship and the crew.[6]

The news that the ship had arrived safely in Ireland was a great relief to those waiting in Bristol. The elusive islands of Brasil had not been discovered but there remained a conviction that there was land far out to the west across the Atlantic Ocean.

Trade between Bristol and Iceland was well established at this time. The outward cargo consisted mainly of cloth and manufactured goods and the return cargo was mainly 'stockfish', a name given to dried cod from the Icelandic shelf. In 1477, a stranger from Genoa visited Iceland and started asking questions of the local people and also of the Bristol captains trading there. He had heard stories that the Bristol vessels were interested in exploring the seas to the west of Iceland. The stranger picked up some curious stories. Bristol men had found a dark red wood floating on the gulf stream which they claimed was from a place they called the Isle of Brasil. They believed that another island called the Isle of the Seven Cities lay further west again. The stranger took due note, he wanted as much information as he could gather. He had ambitions of his own to sail westwards into the Atlantic to try and find a new route to the Orient. His name was Christopher Columbus.

Unlike Columbus most of the Bristol merchants did not harbour romantic notions of a new route to the Indies. They had a more down-to-earth problem in that the powerful Hanseatic League was challenging their right to trade with Iceland for the stockfish. If islands did exist in the western seas then the Bristol fishermen might find new fishing grounds and make their trade independent of the Hanseatic League.

The following year there is a mention of two small ships, the *Trinity* and the *George*, setting sail on the same quest of 'examining and finding a certain island called the Isle of Brasile'. They were loaded with salt, which implies that they hoped to make a good catch of cod. The Bristol records are silent about their fate. Later events indicate that they might in fact have discovered land but the evidence for this claim will be given when more of the story has unfolded. There is no doubt that Bristol merchants were searching the western ocean for land in the decade before Columbus and there is little doubt that the Genoese explorer was well informed of their voyages and intentions.

It was in 1492 that Christopher Columbus made his epic voyage in the *Santa Maria*, with the *Pinta* and *Nina* in convoy. Columbus crossed the Atlantic and made a successful landfall but, as every schoolboy knows, he discovered the West Indies and not the American mainland. He returned to the Caribbean in 1494 and again in 1498 but it was not until this third crossing that Columbus reached the American mainland and even then it was in South America not the north. He could not have imagined that his 1498 landfall was the same landmass as that of the cold northerly latitudes sighted by Bjarni Herjolfsson in 985 and where Lief Eriksson landed in about the year 1000. When Columbus landed on the American mainland in 1498 he knew that in the northern latitudes at least one ship from Bristol had already crossed the Atlantic before him.

In 1495 a Genoese merchant called Giovanni Caboto arrived in Bristol accompanied by his three sons Lewis, Sebastian and Sancius. He became known in England as John Cabot and he obviously knew of the Bristol voyages into the Atlantic sponsored by John Jay in the 1480s. Cabot, like Columbus, was interested in finding land to the west and in March 1496 he obtained letters patent from Henry VII 'to find, discover, and investigate whatsoever islands, countries, regions or provinces … which before this time were unknown to all Christians'. Cabot lost little time and, in the late summer of 1496 he made his first venture into the Atlantic with a single ship. According to the English agent John Day 'his crew confused him, he was short of supplies and ran into bad weather, and he decided to turn back'.

In the next year followed the most important voyage ever made from the port of Bristol. On about 20 May 1497 John Cabot sailed in a three-masted caravel called the *Matthew* with a crew of eighteen seamen. The days stretched to weeks as the *Matthew* with her swelling sail beat ever westward into the setting sun. The noontime sun lay to the south and at night the pole star lay to starboard to guide the sailors as they sailed their wooden vessel onwards through the Atlantic night. The voyage was in midsummer. The longest day came and went with still no sign of land. But on 24 June there was great rejoicing aboard the ship – to the great delight of the sailors the sea abounded with fish but far more significant was that a new coastline appeared on the horizon. The *Matthew* approached the coast and searched for a place to land. John Cabot went ashore and planted the English flag on the new found land. The findings were described in a letter from John Day to Christopher Columbus:

Joseph Manning, *The whale bone*, 1825, watercolour. The whale bone is reputed to have been brought from Newfoundland by John Cabot. Bristol Museums and Art Gallery (M1955)

44

… and they found tall trees of the kind masts are made, and other smaller trees and the country is very rich in grass. In that particular spot, as I told your Lordship, they found a trail which went inland, they saw a site where a fire had been made, they saw manure of animals which they thought to be farm animals, and they saw a stick half a yard long pierced at both ends, carved and painted with brazil, and by such signs as they believe the land to be inhabited. Since he was just with a few people he did not dare advance inland beyond the shooting distance of a cross-bow, and after taking in fresh water he returned to his ship. All along the coast they found many fish like those which in Iceland are dried in the open and sold in England and other countries, and these fish are called in England 'stockfish'; and thus following the shore they saw two forms running on land after the others, but they could not tell if they were human beings or animals; and it seemed to them that there were fields where they thought might also be villages, and they saw a forest whose foliage looked beautiful.[7]

The *Matthew* spent about two weeks exploring the coast to the south. She then headed back to the east and with help of the prevailing winds in the sails she made a landfall in Europe after a crossing of only fifteen days. Cabot's crew confused him again, as they had done the previous year. His landfall was well to the south, in Brittany. This implies either that the skies were never clear enough to measure the sun's altitude or that Cabot was not skilled at finding his latitude. On 6 August Cabot was back in Bristol, by the tenth he was in London telling the king of his new discoveries.

Cabot, like Columbus, was convinced that he had found a shorter route to Asia, and he made another voyage in 1498, this time with five ships. Little is known of the fate of this expedition, one ship returned badly damaged to Ireland and it is thought that Cabot died on the expedition. It was early in the same year (1498) that the Englishman John Day, alias Hugh Say, wrote a letter to the Spanish 'Grand Admiral', none other than Christopher Columbus, with details of the Cabot expedition as quoted above. The letter, written in Spanish, lay undiscovered in the castle of Simancas, central Spain, until 1955. The account adds fascinating details related to the story. It implies that a landfall was made in the Atlantic Ocean by the Bristol men before Cabot and before Columbus. Furthermore Day implies that Columbus knew of this discovery:

It is considered certain that the cape of the said land was found and discovered in the past by the men from Bristol who found 'Brasil' *as your Lordship well knows*. It was called the Island of Brasil, and it is assumed and believed to be the mainland that the men from Bristol found.[8]

Other adventurers followed Cabot and in 1501 three Bristol merchants, Richard Warde, Thomas Assehurst and John Thomas, petitioned Henry VII to set off on a joint expedition with three Portuguese merchants to 'seek out and discover some islands lying in our sphere of influence'. In the same year the Bristol 'Company of Adventurers into the New Found Lands' was formed and was granted letters patent for voyages of discovery and annexation.

The Bristol voyages leave a great many unanswered questions. Where was 'the land found and discovered in times past by the men from Bristol' mentioned in John Day's letter? Was this same land as that found by John Jay's expedition of 1480? Where was the first point on the American coast seen by John Cabot's crew from the *Matthew*? Where did John Cabot first set foot on the American mainland? Is it possible that the new found land was named after Richard Ameryk, Cabot's Bristolian paymaster?

The claim that Cabot was the first European to re-discover the American mainland is perfectly valid. There is no doubt about Cabot's crossing of the Atlantic, but his voyage is not well documented and we have to rely on secondary sources for information; in fact we know more about it from the Spanish records than from the English. The ship's logs, if they ever existed, have not survived. All information is second hand from letters, gossip, speculation and deduction. Cabot realised the possibility of a new sea passage to the Orient, but the Bristol men wanted no more than new fishing grounds for cod. Their voyages are poorly documented. They had no way of finding an accurate longitude and even the latitude of Newfoundland was not recorded.

The voyage of Columbus enjoyed royal sponsorship, it is well documented and it had the glamorous attraction of a new route to the Orient. Columbus used the power of the new printing press to advertise his discoveries, and his son Fernando wrote a biography which was widely read. John Cabot's son Sebastian is thought to have sailed on the *Matthew*, he lived for nearly 60 years after the voyage but at no time did he describe or write up the dramatic events of his father's voyage for posterity. Perhaps the English were jealous and secretive of their new fisheries. Perhaps they thought a new island in the cold Atlantic was no great discovery. But in 1509 Sebastian Cabot did venture to across the Atlantic with two ships and 300 men. He claimed to have sailed the east coast of the American mainland both south and north further than any before him.

The extent of the new continent soon became evident. Sebastian Cabot's account was published many years after the voyage but it is unconvincing and contains anomalies. The geographer Roger Barlow, writing in the sixteenth century when the Spanish treasure ships were carrying their gold back to Spain, summarised the English achievements:

> The New Founde Lande which was fyrst discovered by the marchants of Brystowe … But whereas our Englishe marchantes of Brystowe dyd enterpryse to discover and discovered that parte of the land, if at that season they had folowed toward the equinoctiall, no dowt but they shuld have founde grete riches of gold and perle as other nations hath done sence that time.[9]

It may seem that such a momentous event as the discovery of America is out of place in a parish history. It has been dealt with at some length because there is plenty at St Mary Redcliffe to show the very strong connections between the church and the new world explorations of the late fifteenth century. John Cabot's ship the *Matthew* is reputed to have been built on Redcliffe Wharf and he is supposed to have brought back from Newfoundland the whalebone in the Chapel of St John.

It is impossible to authenticate the whalebone, but nothing could be more authentic than the beautiful double canopied brass in the chancel floor commemorating John Jay with his wife and their fourteen children. But at St Mary Redcliffe there is a third memorial to the exploration of the north Atlantic in these times. Set into the chancel floor is another brass, mentioned earlier, commemorating John Brook who died in 1522 and his wife Johanna. She was the daughter of Richard Ameryk who was the collector of customs at Bristol at the time that Cabot made his great voyage. There are many who believe that America was not named after the Florentine banker Amerigo Vespucci but after Richard Ameryk of St Mary Redcliffe, Bristol. (In 1897 a hitherto unknown roll of accounts was discovered in the archives of Westminster Abbey. It showed that in 1498 one of the collectors of customs at Bristol was called Richard

John Brook died in 1522. He is shown in his legal robes which are similar to those of John Juyn almost 100 years earlier. His wife wears the costume of the time, with Kennel head-dress and on her belt hangs a pomander ball, typical of the period. She was the daughter of Richard Ameryk who paid John Cabot the bounty of King Henry VII upon his return from the voyage of discovery in 1497. This is the source of the claim that the newly-discovered continent was named after Ameryk.

Ameryk. He was the man responsible for the payment of John Cabot's pension.) It is a claim which may well be true but is very difficult to substantiate.[10]

1. Neale p59

2. Neale p73

3. Little pp84-86

4. L Monkton: *The Late Medieval Rebuilding of St Mary Redcliffe, Almost the Richest City in the Middle Ages.* BAA Conference Transactions XIX

5. Neale p263

6. Neale p418

7. Cumming, Skelton and Quinn: *The Discovery of North America*, London 1971, p80

8. Ibid p80

9. E R G Taylor (ed): 'A Brief Summe of Geographie' by Roger Barlow, Hakluyt Soc 2nd series LXIX 1931, p47, pp179-80

10. Ian Wilson: *The Columbus Myth* (1997)

CHAPTER FIVE

Royal Approval

For over five centuries Rush Sunday has been a great occasion at St Mary Redcliffe. It was instituted in 1493 by William Spenser, the mayor of Bristol, and it became a tradition that the mayor and civic dignitaries attended the Rush Sunday service every year at Whitsuntide.

Rush Sunday quickly grew to become a very grand civic and ecclesiastical ceremony. The Mayor (later Lord Mayor) of Bristol, with all the Aldermen of the city wearing their full civic robes, were accompanied by the High Sheriff, the Chief Constable, the City Sword Bearer and other dignitaries. A procession of coaches and horsemen, with each coach accompanied by liveried footmen, left the Mansion House and crossed over Bristol Bridge heralded by the shrill high ringing notes of the official trumpeters. They turned into Redcliffe Street and processed southwards towards the gate in the city wall waving regally to the crowds of people lining the street. Once through the Redcliffe Gate, the procession soon arrived at the north porch of the church. The mayor dismounted from the coach to walk up the grand curved flight of steps to the church. When inside, a brass sword holder was provided to hold the ceremonial sword. Then the mayor and the aldermen were treated to three times the normal ration of sermons. This was not quite what it seems, for the sermons were held on three consecutive days in Pentecost week and it seems unlikely that the mayor and company came to all three.

The church floor was evidently strewn with rushes early in the Middle Ages and the ceremony was to mark the relaying of the floor with fresh rushes once a year in the spring. The Rush Sunday tradition was common in all churches in these early centuries but as more and more of the floors became paved the great majority of churches disbanded the ceremony. St Mary's chose to retain Rush Sunday; however, the number of sermons was reduced from three to one, but the tradition lasted on through the centuries to the present day.

The church of St Mary Redcliffe lay outside the walls of Bristol, but part of the parish lay inside the walls. Temple church, by way of contrast, lay inside the walls but part of its parish lay outside Bristol, in the county of Somerset. By the sixteenth century the population of Bristol had grown to about 6000 and we have figures to show how the population was distributed between the sixteen parishes. St Nicholas' was the most populous parish. South of the Avon St Mary's and St Thomas's vied with each other for second place and in the heart of the city St Ewen's took the wooden spoon with only 56 parishioners. Some of the figures are exact but many, including St Mary Redcliffe, are rounded and can therefore be only approximate:

Population of Bristol Parishes circa 1530

St Werburgh	160	St Stephen	461
St James	520	St Mary Redcliffe	600
St Thomas	600	All Saints	180
St Philip	514	Temple	481
St John	227	St Ewen	56
St Nicholas	800	St Leonard	120
St Peter	400	St Michael	252
Christ Church	326	St Mary-le-Port	180
		Total	5877[1]

The sixteenth century was a very unsettled time for church communities. After the break with Rome under Henry VIII the new Church of England was created as a Protestant religion. When Henry realised that there was a way for him to get his hands on the wealth of the monasteries, there was great trouble to come.

In 1533 Hugh Latimer was a country parson in Wiltshire. He rose to become the Bishop of Worcester where he preached provocative revolutionary sermons from the pulpit. The Dominican and Franciscan Friars objected to his teachings and their representative, Edward Powell, was sent to Bristol to denounce Latimer's teachings from the pulpit of the church of St Thomas. When Henry divorced Catherine of Aragon, Powell sided with the deposed queen. He also sympathised with Mary Queen of Scots but he became too outspoken in his views and in 1535 he was arrested and held in the Tower of London. He was executed in July 1540.

When Anne Boleyn was queen she took a particular interest in St John's Hospital at Redcliffe and she insisted on appointing the next master of the hospital when the post became vacant. In 1542 she appointed David Hutton, a Bristol grocer who had served

The Geneva Bible was published in English in 1577 by Protestant scholars in Geneva. It showed Adam and Eve as having made 'breeches' to cover their nakedness, this caused it to become known as the 'breeches bible'.
It was an important influence on the King James Bible of 1611.

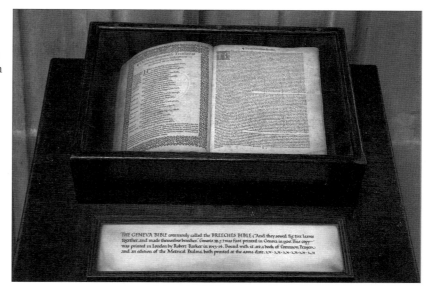

as sheriff, to the vacancy. His appointment lasted only two years because Henry VIII suppressed the hospital with the monasteries in 1544.[2] The dissolution of the monasteries was effected mainly without incident in Bristol. The nunnery of St Mary Magdalene closed in 1536, the income was a mere £21 per annum supporting only one elderly nun and a young novice. In 1537 and 1538 the four friaries closed, first the Carmelites, then the Franciscans, followed by the Augustinians and finally the Dominicans. In the midst of all the closures came a significant change for the better when, on Lady Day 1543, there was a procession from Christ Church to St Mary Redcliffe and the litany was sung for the first time in English as opposed to Latin. The first English bibles were introduced in 1538 but the earliest surviving English bible at St Mary Redcliffe is a copy of the Geneva Bible published in 1557. The Geneva Bible was the work of English Protestants who fled to Geneva in the Catholic reign of Mary and who worked under the direction of Miles Colverdale, John Knox and John Calvin. It is also known as a 'breeches bible' because it describes Adam and Eve as having made breeches to cover their nakedness in the Garden of Eden.

Many people died for their faith in these troubled times, but in Bristol the number of martyrs was thankfully few. One non-resident Catholic priest was martyred and in the reign of Mary five Protestants were burnt at the stake.[3]

At Redcliffe the two chantries founded by William Canynges were suppressed by an act of Edward VI in 1547. The interior of the Chapel of the Holy Spirit was dismantled in about 1550, probably because it was seen to have papal images, and twenty years

At the foot of the tower in St John's Chapel can be found some of the oldest of the church fabric. The medieval glass is here. There was much destruction during the Civil War but the fragments have been pieced together to show as much as possible of the original designs.

The Palm Sunday window in the south ambulatory. In four pictures it tells the story of Christ's triumphal entry into Jerusalem mounted on a donkey.

later the chapel was restructured as a school. The medieval altars were stripped from the main church and in 1566 the chancel was levelled. There were wall paintings in the church at this time. Considered to be 'superstitious images', they were painted over. The stained glass windows were destroyed at this time and only broken fragments survive in St John's Chapel. This completed the purging of all things 'Popish' from the medieval interior. There are certainly plenty of empty niches at St Mary Redcliffe, particularly around the north porch and the tower. These niches may have been deprived of their statues at this time but it is more likely that the empty niches never got as far as having statues in them.[4]

One important change to come out of the Reformation was the creation of a new diocese and cathedral for Bristol, raising it to the status of a city. St Mary Redcliffe, by far the largest and most beautiful church in the new diocese, was an obvious choice for the cathedral. It was not to be. The new cathedral had to be north of the Avon for it to occupy a central position. St Mary Redcliffe was outside the walls and too far to the south. The Abbey church of St Augustine's was chosen instead. It was an unfortunate choice at the time for the Abbey church was in the process of being rebuilt and the nave had been pulled down. The new diocese was pitifully short of money and for centuries Bristol had to manage with half a church for a cathedral, an anomaly that was not corrected until Victorian times. The first mention of Bristol Cathedral is from the traveller John Leland, writing in 1541:

> The castle and most part of the town by north standeth upon a ground metely eminent betwixt the rivers of Avon and Fraw, alias Frome. There riseth an hill of an notable height in respect of the plot of the town self from Frome bridge on, so goeth up along onto Saint Austin's, alias the Trinitie, the cathedral church, and there endeth.[5]

He also noticed St Mary Redcliffe. He made only a brief comment but it was in some ways the most moving tribute ever made: 'Redcliffe longe pulcherrima omnium ecclesia', or in English simply 'Redcliffe church, the most beautiful of all'.

When Queen Elizabeth ascended to the throne in 1558 the religious situation had at last become more stable. In 1574 the queen made an official state visit to Bristol. She entered the castle grounds through Lafford's Gate where the mayor presented the city's gilt mace to her majesty as a symbol of her sovereignty over Bristol. The queen graciously returned it. The mayor knelt before the queen whilst the recorder, John Popham, delivered a long oration and presented her majesty with a silk purse containing 100 pounds in gold. Then there was a clanging of metal chains as the great barbican gate of the castle was opened and the procession entered the packed streets of Bristol where a cheering multitude of people waited to get a glimpse of their virgin queen. The mayor rode proudly between two sergeants at arms, in front of the queen and her retinue. Then came the common council followed by the nobility and a great fanfare of trumpeters. The procession was very long, at the rear were 400 soldiers in livery, 300 harquebusiers and 100 pikemen attired in white corselettes.

It was well known that Elizabeth loved pageants and Bristol was determined not to disappoint her. A great wooden fort had been constructed by the quay with a smaller fort standing on the hill beyond, both built especially for the queen so that a great military drama could be enacted for her to enjoy. A timber scaffolding was built in the Marsh to enable the queen and spectators to get a grandstand view of the proceedings. The smaller fort was taken in the first day but the larger fort was assaulted from land and water in a mock battle that lasted for four days. The queen then had to listen to boring speeches and bad poetry which she suffered without complaint. The military experiment cost a fortune in gunpowder but Good Queen Bess was well pleased with it. There is no doubt that she thoroughly enjoyed her visit and the hospitality of the people and she 'gave Mr Maior and his brethren greate thankes for theire doinges'.

The queen's vantage point was situated in what later became Queen Square. Thus, for several days, she could not help but notice the very beautiful gothic church with its pinnacles and flying buttresses standing against the Redcliffe skyline.

Elizabeth is said to have described the church of St Mary's as 'the fairest, goodliest, and most famous parish church in all England' – a remark which has come to epitomise St Mary Redcliffe.

Did Queen Elizabeth really make this flattering compliment? The only way to prove beyond doubt that the words belong to her would be from a record written in her own hand or from somebody very close to her at the time. But a few years later another Tudor visitor, William Camden, also witnessed St Mary Redcliffe for the first time. Camden's account actually was published so that we know exactly the words he used:

> Among the fairest of the latter [churches] is St Mary de Redcliffe, without the walls, with a grand ascent of steps, the whole so spacious and well built, with an arched roof of stone and a lofty steeple, as to exceed, in my opinion, all the parish churches of England that I have yet seen...[6]

Both Queen Elizabeth and Camden seemed to be completely unconcerned about the truncated spire. Notice the mention of a 'grand ascent of steps' up the slope of the hill to the north porch. Some of the early pictures show a fine curved sweeping staircase with a stone balustrade. Camden's remarks are so similar to those attributed to the queen that it is quite possible, over a period of time, that they have been mistakenly attributed to her. A third version, with almost the same wording, has been attributed to Charles I in the following century, 'the parish church of Redcliffe for the foundation structures and buildings thereof is one of the moste famous, absolute fayrest and goodliest parish churches within the Realm of England'. What then are we to believe about Queen Elizabeth's remarks? It may be said that William Camden was one of the few people in England who had travelled more than the queen and his opinion may be of greater value, but of course his remarks do not hold the same charisma as those of England's virgin queen. If, at the time of her visit, the queen had been asked to give her opinion of the church then her words would surely have been very similar to those

A homely wooden carving of Queen Elizabeth I with orb and sceptre. Elizabeth is reputed to have described St Mary Redcliffe as 'the fairest, goodliest and most famous parish church in England.' It probably dates from the opening of the parish school in 1571 and is now in St John's Chapel.

actually attributed to her. Whilst we will never have absolute proof of her exact words, the story remains, like Drake finishing his game of bowls on Plymouth Hoe, as a minor embellishment of what is basically the truth. There is little to be gained by being finicky about the precise words. The story can be accepted as correct in principle. St Mary Redcliffe certainly deserves the compliment attributed to Queen Elizabeth and it will remain forever as an integral part of the church history.

One of the Elizabethan gems in the church is the carved wooden effigy of Queen Elizabeth herself, fully robed and holding the orb and sceptre in her hands. It has been suggested that the carving was made to be the figurehead of a Tudor ship, but if this is true it did not have to suffer the salty rigours of a ship's figurehead for long because it is too well preserved. The figure has a simple appeal about it, and the likeness bears little resemblance to the official haughty portraits of Elizabeth painted by the royal court painters. Elizabeth wears a crown and a Tudor ruff but she has a homely expression of concern and benevolence. This is the face of Good Queen Bess. The carving of Elizabeth is very old and it may predate the queen's visit to Bristol for it is reasonable to suggest that it dates from the founding of the parish school in 1571. The school was known by the name of 'Queen Elizabeth's Free Grammar and Writing School'. It was to have a master and an under master and to be governed by twelve 'discreet and honest men'. The school is well documented and it was housed in the detached Chapel of the Holy Spirit which stood near the southwest corner of the church close to the boundary with Redcliffe Hill. The building was no longer used as a chapel in Queen Elizabeth's reign for the records show that the altar was removed in 1550 and the choir screen in 1553. It therefore provided an ideal location for the new school.

In 1583 the Redcliffe road was in a bad state of repair. A drummer set up on Redcliffe Hill to rally the local people to carry the stones to repair the road. The work was unpaid but their reward came four months later when the mayor and company arrived at Redcliffe church stile and served the

Children of Redcliffe have been baptised in this octagonal stone font since the fifteenth century.

workers with beer, paid for out of the corporation funds. This incident may well have taken place during the annual perambulation of the city boundaries by the mayor and aldermen in their best fineries, a ceremonial event which attracted a crowd of scampering children. The council records for 1584 mention a breakfast for the mayor and sheriffs where cakes and seven quarts of wine were consumed. After the shire stones had all been duly visited an afternoon of drinking disposed of a gallon of 'Mathera' at four pence per pint and 1s 4d was 'paid to the labourers to make the ways open.'[7]

Later in the 1580s Redcliffe became involved with preparations for the invasion of the Spanish Armada. In 1586 there was a grand inspection of the troops by the Lord-Lieutenant of Bristol and Somerset, the Earl of Pembroke with his guard of 32 horsemen, and he was met by a salute of 32 cannon. The meeting place was at Addercliffe, the cliffs on the site of Redcliffe Parade. A second mustering was held the following year when the meeting point was Redcliffe church. On this occasion a large red banner

The richly carved Eizabethan parish chest from 1593. The chest was lost for many years but rediscovered in Bath in 1881. The carved wording 'Commune ye one with another' and 'Sainte Marie Redclyfe Bristole' left no doubt about its authenticity.

was produced made from 37 yards of taffeta.[8]

Celebrations and thanksgiving services were held everywhere after the defeat of the Spanish Armada in 1588. A survival from this period is the Redcliffe parish chest of carved oak in the late Tudor style. The front panels are beautifully carved in the Elizabethan manner depicting faith, hope and charity with the words 'Commune ye one with another' and the bottom rail inscribed 'Sainte Marie Redclyfe Bristole. 1593'. The chest has a mini history of its own: it disappeared for many years after being removed from the church and nobody knew what had become of it. In 1881 it was discovered in Bath and it was returned to its original place in the Chatterton room above the north porch.

1. Latimer XVI p25

2. Latimer XVI p31

3. KG Powell: *The Marion Martyrs*: Bristol branch of the Historical Association 1972

4. Drury: p212

5. L T Smith (ed): *The Itineraries of John Leland 1535-43*, V, 1910 pp86-93

6. R Gough (ed): *William Camden s Britannia 1586*

7. Latimer XVI p79

8. Latimer XVI pp80 and 90

CHAPTER SIX

The Puritans

In the early years of the seventeenth century Bristol lived through two disasters. In 1607, after an exceptionally wet January, the river Severn broke its banks and the whole of the valley from Gloucester to Bristol was flooded. Five hundred lives were lost in this disaster. Redcliffe Street and Temple Street were under several feet of water. St Mary Redcliffe was fortunate to be built on the hill and to escape the worst of the flooding. The flooding of the farm land meant that the harvest for 1607 was a disaster and this put further hardship on the poor.

The flood and the famine were natural disasters, but for the next generation worse was to come as the country moved towards Civil War. When war broke out between Charles I and his Parliament the City of Bristol declared for Parliament. There was a strong Puritanical faction in Bristol and most of those involved in trade supported Parliament against the king. But there were also significant numbers declaring for the Royalists so that the city was by no means in complete agreement about which side to support. In 1642 a contingent of 300 men was raised with four small guns. It was agreed to fit out three ships for the defence of Bristol. The city walls were 400 years old. They had been built at a time when gunpowder was unknown and they were designed for a much smaller city in an age when assaults were made with bows and arrows, spears and catapults. St Mary Redcliffe had always been outside the walls to the south but much of Bristol had also spread beyond the walls to the north so that the bridges over the Frome, rather than the wall to the south, were seen as the weakest points at which to launch an assault against Bristol.

Colonel Nathaniel Fiennes arrived as military commander to the Bristol garrison. Situated as it was in the West Country, Bristol was surrounded by neighbouring towns mostly supporting the Royalists and it was therefore only a question of time before the city came under siege. There was concern over the Royalist sympathisers inside Bristol and rumours were spread of plots to betray the city and to let in Prince Rupert and his troops overnight by stealth. Notable amongst the Royalist plotters were William Colston, George Boucher, Robert Yeamans and his brother William, along with some of the clergy. The Yeamans family was closely connected with St Mary Redcliffe as were probably some of the others. Their plans were discovered and the plotters were brought to trial. In May 1643 George Boucher and Robert Yeamans were executed but Yeamans' brother William was acquitted.[1]

The Royalists arrived in strength from all directions to take Bristol. On the river Avon eight armed ships appeared to give them support and to take on the three parliamentary ships. Ralph Hopton arrived from the west with his Royalist Cornish troops under Lord Hertford. Prince Rupert set up his headquarters at Westbury-on-Trym and he planned to attack Bristol from the Royal Fort. There followed the famous charge from

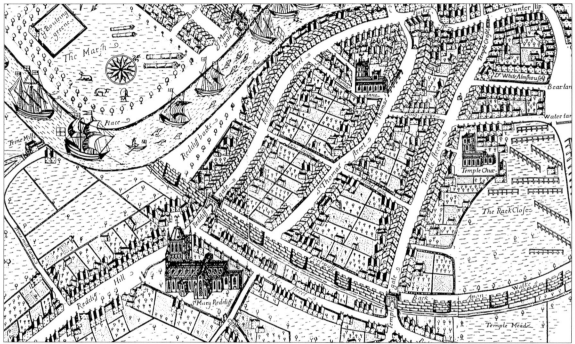

Millerd's map of 1673 shows every house and field and St Mary Redcliffe standing outside the city walls.

a point near the top of Park Street where Henry Washington, a distant forbear of George Washington, routed the defenders and took Bristol by storm. In the south however, the medieval defences held and the Cornish troops were unable to scale the solid thirteenth-century wall. There was much local fighting and looting, and Redcliffe church was fortunate to escape with minimal loss and damage.

Thus, Bristol became a Royalist stronghold. The Royalists were euphoric after taking Bristol and there was even talk of moving the King's court from Oxford. But elsewhere the war was going badly for them and in the months following they had little to shout about. The turning point was the battle of Marston Moor in 1644. The war lasted another year but the end was imminent after the battle of Naseby in June 1645. Prince Rupert retreated back to Bristol and the city was soon under siege a second time, but this time the parties were reversed and it was the Parliamentarians who were on the offensive. When Bristol was besieged by the Roundheads, Bedminster was one of the places burnt to the ground by the Cavaliers so that the besiegers were denied food and shelter from that quarter. In September 1645 Rupert surrendered.

In the years that followed under Cromwell's protectorate, the Puritans came to rule the country. The lavish style and the outstanding architecture of St Mary Redcliffe

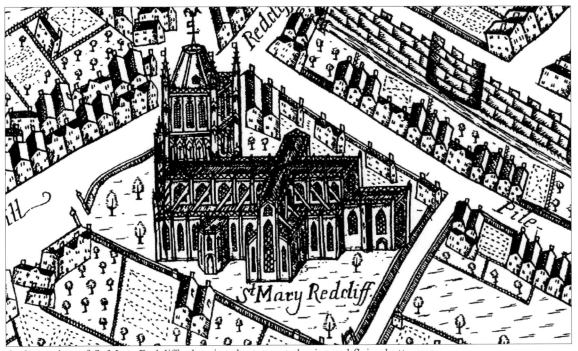

A closer view of St Mary Redcliffe showing the truncated spire and flying buttresses.

could hardly have shown a greater contrast with the frugal furnishings of the Puritan church and this is no doubt one reason why very little in terms of lavish church memorials can be found for this period. It would seem, however, that the church fabric and many statues survived and this may well be due to the continuing support that the church enjoyed from the wealthy leading citizens of Bristol. During the common-wealth years the Puritanical policies gradually built up resentment amongst the common people; much good was done in suppressing blood sports but a lot of harm was done in denying the people their simple pleasures at times such as Easter and Christmas. Even the water conduit near the west wall, where the women normally exchanged gossip and joked happily as they drew the water, was banned from use on the Sabbath.

By a magisterial ordinance, all the conduits in the city were kept closed throughout the Sabbath day, and the parish constables were required to lay information against persons carrying water to their homes, in order that the culprits might be brought up on Monday and duly punished. Still another forbade the plying of the ferry at Temple Back on the Lord's Day. William Hobson, a cousin to Edward Colston, was sent to prison for six months and required to find securities for his future behaviour for having said, perhaps in joke, that drunkenness was not a sin. Many games and holiday amusements were interdicted, and though some of the sports, such as cock throwing, dog-fighting, and bull bating, were cruel and deserved to be put down, it was strongly suspected that they were forbidden, not because they gave pain to animals, but because they gave pleasure to the spectators. Maypoles entirely disappeared, and finally by a Parliamentary decree, Christmas Day was appointed as a national fast.[2]

It was the killjoy attitude of the Puritans, as much as anything else, that caused them to lose popularity and it was hardly surprising that the people wanted back their maypoles, their harvest festivals and their Christmas celebrations.

In the 1650s the Civil War was over but a conflict with the Dutch had broken out. Admiral Blake won a naval victory over the Dutch in the English Channel and he arrived in Bristol with fifty Dutch prisoners who had to be accommodated somewhere in the city. The castle dungeons were no longer safe and the prisoners were, therefore, held in the crypt of St Mary Redcliffe. Fifty mats were purchased at 1s 4d each for the prisoners of war to sleep on. The church became a gaol for several months until, at the end of 1655, the prisoners were transferred from Bristol to Chepstow Castle.

After the restoration of the monarchy in 1660 things improved rapidly. Humphrey Brent was appointed as vicar in 1660 and Richard Thompson, a man notorious for his sermons, followed him in 1678. It became much safer to travel and sightseers became more frequent. We are fortunate to have several first-hand accounts from visitors of this period. In between the Dutch wars in the summer of 1662, William Schellinks arrived from Amsterdam and he travelled by boat down the Avon, for he had heard of the efficacy of the waters at Hotwells and was eager to sample them. He listed all the churches of Bristol, numbering nineteen at the time and he made special mention of St Mary's:

Redcliffe Church lies above the harbour called the Quay on a small height, built there by a merchant of Bristol. It is a glorious building, but the towers were not completed when he died, and on one the spire is half built. His tomb can be seen in the corner to the right hand side of the choir, where his wife's carved effigy lies.[3]

He goes on to name the merchant as William Canynges and he quotes the figures from Rikart's *Kalendar*, the same figures quoted by William Worcestre, for Canynges' ships and workmen. He implies that the church was planned with two spires at the west end, as seen at Wells cathedral. It has been suggested that the original plans may have been for twin towers, but these plans were over three centuries old when Schellinks visited. Perhaps in the 1660s there were some who still remembered that the second tower had once been an option and even some who still had ambitions to see it built.

In the same year came Thomas Fuller, a scholar and an Anglican divine who is best known for his notable work *The Worthies of England*. From 1634 to 1641 Fuller had been rector of Broadwindsor in Dorset, within the diocese of Bristol, so he therefore knew Bristol and its cathedral very well. Fuller thought that St Mary Redcliffe should have been chosen as the cathedral for Bristol:

> Redcliffe church in this city clearly carrieth away the credit from all parish churches in England…most stately the ascent thereunto by many stairs, which at last plentifully recompenseth their pains who climb them up, with the magnificent structure both without and within.[4]

Another account survives from about 1670. It has never been published outside the parish magazine, but it is thought to have been written by an anonymous Frenchman. It confirms that visitors were welcome to wander all over the church, up the stairways and even stroll along the roof:

> In this quarter are three large streets, where are some rich merchants and a very beautiful church of Our Lady of Redcliff, for many figures of the saints, and the sculptures in low relief which are all around the church. The steeple of it is high and of very good workmanship: one can walk on the roof of the church which is flat bordered by a balustrade.[5]

The memorial to Sir William Penn, Kt. On the tablet is the obituary written by
his son, William Penn the younger. '… with a gentle & even gale in much peace
arrived & anchored in his Last and Best Port, at Wanstead in ye County of Essex
ye 16 Sept 1670 being then but 49 & 4 months old.'

William Penn, by Sir Peter Lely. St Mary Redcliffe has a close connection with Pennsylvania, one of the 13 original states of the American Union and named after the Quaker, William Penn the elder, who worshipped at St Mary's and was buried here.

We are fortunate to be able to quote a fourth account from the same century, this time a feminine point of view. Celia Fiennes was the daughter of Nathaniel Fiennes, the Parliamentary governor of Bristol during the Civil War. She was an intrepid traveller and in the 1680s she rode side-saddle throughout the whole of England. She left behind her very readable accounts of every place she visited. Miss Fiennes does not actually name the church she is describing, but there is no doubt that it is St Mary Redcliffe. She climbed the 150 steps to the top of the tower and gave a marvellous description of the views across Bristol:

> There is one church which is an entire work all of stone, noe timbers but the rafters and beames belonging to the roofe and the seates they sit in, the leads are very high and large and very neate kept, the tower 150 steppes up, on which the whole Citty is discover'd which by reason of the good gardens and grounds within its walls is a very large tract of ground in the whole; there you can see the Colledge Green in which stands the Cathedrall and the Doctors houses which are not very fine built of stone; there are some few monuments in this church with good carvings of stone round the tombs and some effigies, there are 8 bells in this Church, there is 2 men goes to the ringing the biggest bell.[6]

The earliest of the bells dated from 1622, two decades before the Civil War broke out, and in 1636 there is a record of six bells being re-hung. There are parallels between Celia Fiennes' one hundred and fifty steps to the top of the tower and the eighty steps counted two centuries earlier by William Worcestre to reach the roof level. There are other parallels between the two different centuries and the exploration of the new continent across the Atlantic. Since the voyage of the *Mayflower* in 1620 there had been great developments in the continent where Cabot had made a landfall. Bristol and the west coast ports were at the forefront of these developments. At Kingroad in the Severn estuary the round-bellied high-prowed wooden-walled sailing ships, that had braved the journey across the North Atlantic, rolled at anchor in the swell and waited for the pilot and the next tide to take them along the Avon to the quaysides of Bristol. Every day with every tide there were emotional scenes on the dockside. There were sailors cheerfully returning from distant places with souvenirs and tales of far away lands. There were sailors making their tearful goodbyes to wives and children.

There were also sailors from the Royal Navy who had fought for king and country in the Dutch wars. Members of the Penn family were amongst the latter.

The Penn family became very involved with the development of the American colonies. Giles Penn, in the early decades of the century, was a Bristol merchant and his son William Penn (1621–70) served in the navy. William rose to the rank of admiral during the Dutch wars. For a short time he was imprisoned in the Tower of London for plotting to restore the monarchy. His views on the Restoration eventually prevailed, and he was on the ship *Naseby* in 1660 when Charles II returned to England to claim his throne. Admiral William Penn was a great supporter of the king, he had become very wealthy through his father's business and he invested large sums of money in colonial development. Eventually the king was so much in debt to Admiral Penn that there was only one way for him to pay off the debt. William Penn the younger was granted a tract of land of about sixty square miles near the Delaware River in America. The place became known as Pennsylvania. The name was subsequently applied to a whole state, reaching from the Delaware River in the east right across to Lake Eire in the west, some 300 miles long and 140 miles wide between two parallels of latitude.

William Penn the elder is buried at St Mary Redcliffe. He died in 1670: his burial place is in the south transept and his funeral armour and memorial are displayed in the nave near the rear of the church. William Penn the elder is frequently confused with his son. William Penn the younger was the first governor of the new state of Pennsylvania. The younger Penn was very keen to ensure that the colonists had the religious freedom to interpret the gospel as they saw fit. In particular he wanted the Quakers to follow their own religion in the British colonies. His wishes were accepted and Pennsylvania became the stronghold of Quakerism in the New World.

The new colony was originally formed by English Quakers from the Bristol area, but they were soon joined by Swedish, German and Swiss families eager to partake in the new freedom. The fact that Pennsylvania was named after the father and not the son is proved by a letter from William Penn the younger dated 5 January 1681. He honoured his father who had been dead for ten years but he felt it was very pretentious to use the Penn family name for the new colony. King Charles over-ruled him and pushed it through by Royal assent. A private letter describes Penn's feelings on the matter:

Above the south door are the coat of arms of Charles II, who was instrumental in the founding of the state of Pennsylvania.

Dear Friend,

… after many waitings, watchings, solicitings, and disputes in council, this day my country was confirmed to me under the great seal of England, with large powers and privileges, by the name of Pennsylvania; a name the king would give it in honour of my father …

[I proposed]… Sylvania, and they added Penn to it, and though I was much opposed to it, and went to the king to have it struck out and altered, he said it was past, and would take it upon him; nor could twenty guineas move the under secretary to vary the name; for I feared lest it be looked upon as a vanity in me, and not as a respect in the King, as it truly was, to my father, whom he often mentions with praise …

Thy true friend,

Wm Penn[7]

It is an astonishing fact therefore, that the church of Redcliffe was not only connected with the first voyages of discovery into the Atlantic Ocean but it was also involved with the expansion of the American Colonies. The wealth and grandeur of the church attracted the merchant venturers to support it, and the merchants were prepared to put much of their wealth toward the high upkeep of the church fabric and the running of the church. But Redcliffe, like every other parish in the country, was still responsible for the poor of the parish and it is not until this time, parish registers excepted, that we are able to find written records of these humbler people. The church accounts from 1690/91 show the payments made to the poor in that year; over forty names are mentioned, local people from the grass roots of the parish:

An account of the parochial payment of charity made by John Gibbes ... of the parish of St Mary Redcliffe of the poor ... Given weekly from the seventh month of 1690 TO

Widow Lyner	1s	0d	Jone Bush	0s	6d
Lettis Williams	0s	8d	Hawkin's child	1s	6d
Widow Wells	0s	8d (died)	Peises 2 children	2s	4d
Widow Chelve	(given to the children)		Whitles child	1s	0d
Widow Bartlet	1s	4d	Pople's 2 children	2s	4d
Widow Hix	0s	6d	Widow Griffin	1s	0d
Widow Attkins	0s	6d	Dutch woman	1s	0d
Widow Jones	0s	8d	Thomas Gof	1s	0d
Widow Evans	1s	0d (died)	Widow Fletcher	0s	6d (died)
Dibbin's child	1s	6d	Larfor's 2 children	2s	6d
Griffon's child	1s	6d	Goody Allen	0s	6d
Gennut's child	1s	6d	Royers's child	1s	4d
Widow Toby	1s	6d	Andrew Perkins	1s	0d
Widow Leech	0s	6d	Barker's boy	0s	8d
Edward Collins	1s	0d	Goody Broad	1s	0d
Elizabeth May	1s	0d	John Humphreys	1s	0d
Thomas Evans	5s	0d[8]	Goodman Owen	0s	6d
Widow Port	0s	6d	Pople's boy	1s	4d
Mary Chelve	0s	0d (died)	Goodman Jennings	0s	6d
Marjorie West	0s	10d	Widow Bush	1s	0d
Widow Stanford	0s	4d	Grace Watkins	1s	0d (died)
Widow Heath	0s	6d (died)	Widow Leaves	1s	0d
Widow Wolfreed	1s	0d	Thomas Evans	5s	0d[8]
Mary Green	1s	6d			

Payments were made weekly and accounted by John Gibbes, the overseer of the poor (not to be confused with John Gibb who became vicar of Redcliffe twelve years later).

The records cover six months and six of the recipients died in the 26-week period of the accounts. The list includes a great many widows and orphaned children. It is useful in identifying the names of many of the families in Redcliffe at this time and therefore supplementing the data in the parish register. Redcliffe was in some respects a rural parish, differing from the inner city parishes such as All Saints and St Ewen's with their tightly defined parish boundaries. In other respects it was similar to the city centre parishes, in that the families did not often remain for longer than one or two generations. The continual influx of fresh blood was a good thing but the downside was that, where many rural parishes can trace the names of local families for many generations, this was seldom the case at St Mary Redcliffe.

1. Little p127

2. Latimer XVII p254

3. Exwood and Lehmann (eds): *Journals of William Schellinks Travels in England 1661-63* (1993) p103

4. Thomas Fuller: *The Worthies of England* (1952 edition) pp504-510

5. PM Feb 1932

6. Christopher Morris (ed): *The Journeys of Celia Fiennes*

7. CM MacInnes: *Bristol, A Gateway of Empire*, chapter 6

8. BRO P/StMR/OP/4

CHAPTER SEVEN

Music, Art and Industry

The new vicarage was built on Redcliffe Hill very early in the eighteenth century. It was a beautiful house in the new Queen Anne style. The old vicarage was also on Redcliffe Hill, a substantial house but of no great architectural merit and one of a picturesque row of gabled houses which comprised Redcliffe Hill in the seventeenth century. The new vicar, John Gibb, who had served as a prebendary since 1697, took up residence when the new vicarage was completed in 1702.

In 1707 the vestry obtained a royal mandate to make a collection throughout the parishes of England to support a costly restoration of the church fabric. Nearly two thousand pounds was raised by this method. In addition to the money from the mandate there was other income available to improve the church furnishings and plenty of high-quality improvements were made at this time. The first improvement was the restoration of the south wall and the south entrance porch carried out from 1708 to 1710. The finest artisans were employed to beautify the interior of the church. A good example is the set of ornate iron gates built originally as a screen for the chancel and gates to the north and south aisles. They are the work of William Edney. The brass eagle lectern was a gift from James Wathen, a Bristol pin maker; it belonged to the previous century and was donated in 1638, a few years before the Civil War broke out.

The next major investment in the church was a grand new organ. A reference is made to repairing an organ in 1611 so the new instrument was therefore not the first in the church. No details of the early organ are known but it was probably a fairly simple instrument and it was replaced with something much more imposing. The finest organ builders of the age, Harris and Byfield, were commissioned to build the new organ for the church. Completed in 1726, it had very fine acoustic qualities and resonated beautifully in the high roof of the church. It had 26 stops and 1928 pipes, it stood 53 feet high, almost touching the roof, and was highly decorated in the style of the times. It was modelled as a triumphal Roman arch and was crowned with pinnacles and winged angels. Amongst its innovations it had what is reputed to be the first octave coupler. It was situated at the back of the church near the west door.

A few years after the organ was installed a new vicar, the Rev. Thomas Broughton –

William Edney's iron gates of 1710, separating the box pews from the west end of the church. Edney was the foremost craftsman in wrought iron of his time.

author of *Dictionary of all religions* – took up residence in the vicarage. He was married to Anne Harris, daughter of the Rev. Thomas Harris, and the vicarage became a family home, for she bore the vicar six children. There is a tradition that one of the most honoured guests at the vicarage was the German composer George Frederick Handel. It was rumoured that Handel was in financial difficulties and trying to evade his creditors at this time. How could Handel resist playing the new organ? The English public were not great enthusiasts of Handel's Italian operas and it seems out of keeping to play these in a church, but everybody loved the *Water Music* and the twelve *Chandos Anthems* which he was composing at the time. It has been suggested that in the 1720s this music flowed out into the nave of St Mary Redcliffe, created by the hand of the composer himself. Handel's libretto for the oratorio *Hercules* was actually written for his friend the vicar. Careful research by Maurice Fells casts doubt on the authenticity of the story, as he was unable to find any reference to Handel's visit to Bristol. The stained-glass Handel memorial window proves nothing, as it was not

The lectern dates from 1638. It was given to the church by James Wathen who was the churchwarden and a pin maker by trade.

installed until the nineteenth century, long after the event. The window depicts the traditional Christmas story of the shepherds abiding in the fields at night. The fact that Handel was a friend of Thomas Broughton is true, however, and goes some way towards authenticating the Handel connection.[1]

The organ makes occasional appearances in the eighteenth-century parish records. Nelme Rogers was organist from 1727 to 1772 and he was followed by John Allen. There is also a reference to an unknown 'Broderip' who was not quite as accomplished as Rogers and Allen:

The house of foolish cits and drunken boys
Offends my ears, like Broderips horrid noise;
While Broderip's hum drum symphonies of flats
Rival the harmony of midnight cats.

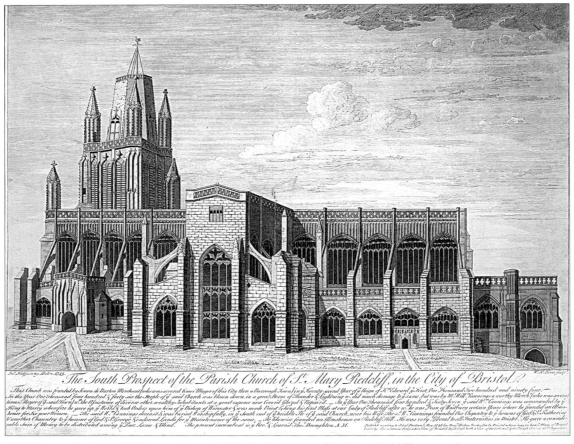

The South Prospect of the Parish Church of S.t Mary Redcliff, in the City of Bristol.

W H Toms after John Halfpenny, drawn 1745, *South prospect of St Mary Redcliffe*, engraving, Bristol Museums and Art Gallery (M1601).

John Allen's playing is described by the same critic:

> How unlike Allen! Allen is divine!
>
> His touch is sentimental, tender, fine;
>
> No little affection's 'ere disgraced
>
> Hid more refined, his sentimental taste.
>
> He keeps the passions with the sound in play,
>
> And the soul trembles with the trembling key.
>
> *Thomas Chatterton*

The altar was next in line for upgrading. It was decided that a work of art by one of the great masters would be appropriate for this improvement:

It was agreed that the Altar-Piece of the Parish Church of St Mary Redcliffe be new painted and that an Application be made to Mr Hogarth to know whether he will undertake to paint the same and to desire him to come from London to survey and make an estimate thereof...[2]

E Kirkall after John Strahan, *The organ at the west end*, engraving, Bristol Museums and Art Gallery (Mb6683).

The new altar piece was to be a triptych, a painting in three parts. William Hogarth agreed to do the paintings and Thomas Paty, a Bristol architect with a growing reputation, was commissioned to design and make the frames. Paty also designed the new font. In the meantime Hogarth came from London to measure the space around the altar. He returned to London and spent many hard months working at the painting. When the marvellous triptych arrived it was a masterpiece and every inch a Hogarth. But alas! The triptych was too large for the space allocated to it. It was too wide and could only be clumsily displayed with the side pieces set at an angle. The triptych was removed by the Victorians who were unsympathetic to the Grand Manner, and after several moves around the city now resides in the former St Nicholas church by Bristol Bridge.

The bells also had to be upgraded. In 1763 Thomas Bilbie, a bellfounder of Chew Stoke, recast the four middle bells which were cracked and out of tune. During all the upgrading of the church, however, there were bound to be some losses. The Chapel of the Holy Spirit had not been used to hold services since Elizabethan times. It had been restructured to accommodate the school and the prevailing view was that 'the beauty and magnificence of the church were greatly impaired by the situation of the [said] school house'. In 1759 the school was in great decay and the governors dismissed the schoolmaster, the Rev. Thomas Harris, because, they claimed, he had neglected his duties: this in spite of the fact that the vicar was married to the schoolmaster's

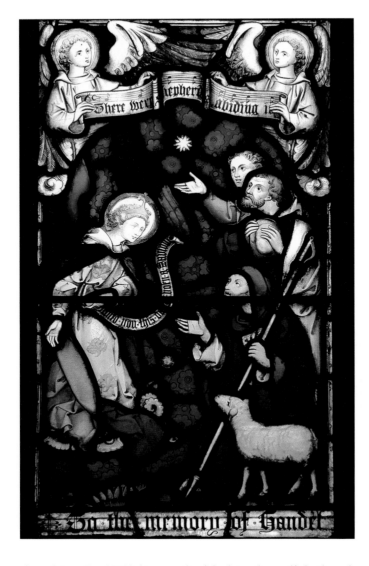

The Handel window was made in his memory 100 years after the composer's death.
It contains words and music from the *Messiah*.

Opposite: Detail of Hogarth's triptych for the altar – for which he was paid £525. Photo: Stephen Morris

daughter. In 1762 it was decided to demolish the chapel and to move the school to the very grand location of the Lady Chapel and to appoint the Rev. Mr Hayward as the new schoolmaster. The Lady Chapel became less sumptuously furnished when it became used as a school and it was actually walled off so that the school did not interfere with the rest of the church. It was a sad day when the old Chapel of the Holy Spirit was pulled down, however, for it was the only survivor of the Early English church from the thirteenth century about which we know so little.

Visitors to Bristol were still plentiful in the eighteenth century. Daniel Defoe repeated the usual story about William Canynges and then was moved to poetry to express his feelings about the church:

No Age nor Time can wear out well-won Fame,

The Stones themselves a stately Work doth show;

From senseless Stones we ground may Mens good name,

And noble Minds by virtuous Deeds we know.

A Lanthorne clear sets forth a Candle-Light;

A worthy act declares a worthy Wight.

The Buildings rare that here you may behold:

To shrine his bones deserves a Tomb of Gold...[3]

The money spent on improvements at this time far exceeded the parish collections. Where did all the money came from? The stock answer is that it came from trade. Bristol had expanded to become the second largest city in the kingdom. The American Colonies were flourishing. Trade was booming everywhere. There was plenty of money available towards the beautification of all the Bristol churches. There was also manufacture. In Redcliffe one manufacturing process in particular was booming.

When Daniel Defoe arrived in 1720 he could hardly miss it.

…There are no less than fifteen glass-houses in Bristol, which is more than there are in the city of London: they have indeed a very great expence of glass bottles, sending them fill'd with beer, cyder, and wine to the West Indies, much more than goes from London; also great numbers of bottles, even such as is almost incredible, are now used for sending the waters of St Vincent's Rock away, which are now carry'd, not all over England only, but, we may say, over all the world.[4]

The fire engine 'with 60 foot of leather hose and brass screws'.

The glass industry was booming in Redcliffe, with one of the kilns practically on the doorstep of the church. The two main ingredients in glass manufacture were sand and coal. Bedminster had coal beneath the ground but it was still many years before it was mined. Bristol had a flourishing coal industry however, centred around the Kingswood area and near enough to supply large quantities to the glass industry.

Sand was available from the Redcliffe caves in what was effectively another mining industry, not as deep and dark and dangerous as the coal mines but underground and dangerous enough in an age of atrocious safety regulations. Defoe counted fifteen glasshouses in 1720, but a decade later they had grown to exceed the number of church spires in Bristol and already the grime and pollution were affecting the stonework of the church. Defoe noted that bottles and window glass were the staple product of the industry but as the glass manufacture progressed and diversified, beautiful artistic pieces gave Bristol glass a world-wide reputation.

It was at about this time that St Mary Redcliffe purchased a parish fire engine, an unusual item for a church but one which indicates that there was a real fear of fire spreading from the nearby industrial sites to the church. The receipt is dated 1760 'to a new engine with 60 foot of leather hose and brass screws'. The cost was forty-five pounds but the old engine was traded in for ten pounds so there was evidently a parish fire engine for at least a few decades before 1760. The engine, which still survives and is on display in the south aisle, consists of a wooden box with four solid wooden wheels, a length of hose to take water from the river or a pond and a handle for the hefty fire fighters to pump the water by hand. It was a slow process: first the water had to be pumped from the nearest supply to fill the box, then it had to be carted manually to the fire, as there were no shafts for horses. Only then could the water be pumped through the hoses to extinguish the fire.[5]

At the Bristol Record Office there survives a list of the benefactors to what was known as the Yeamans', White's and Edson's charity. This money was used to help the sick and the poor of the parish.

YEAMANS' WHITE'S AND EDSON'S CHARITY DONATIONS 1647–1756

1662 Mrs Ann Edson	1641 Thomasine Harrington
1662 Mr Richard Luckcock	1650 George Gibbs
1685 Mr Jeremiah Holloway	1654 John Haytor
1686 Mr Samuel Hale	1675 Joseph Bullock
1689 Mr John Lawford	1686 Robert Yeamans
1756 Ann White	1691 Susanna Compton
1631 Richard Vickeris (Alderman)	1719 William James
1632 Robert Rogers (Alderman)	1721 Ann Tilly
1635 Richard Rogers	1724 John Newman[6]

We cannot leave the times without mentioning another industry, one which in the middle and later decades of the eighteenth century created great wealth for some in Bristol. This was of course the years of the transatlantic slave trade which until the 1990s was embarrassingly ignored by Bristol historians. There is no doubt every church in Bristol profited, to a greater or lesser extent, by this horrific trade of human cargoes. There is a story that in 1791 when the bill to abolish slavery was defeated in the House of Commons, the bells of St Mary Redcliffe rang out to celebrate the occasion. This story is unlikely to be true for the church accounts for the time have been studied and there is no mention of a payment to the bell ringers on this occasion.

James Johnson, *View from the north transept to the south transept with the Canynges monument in the distance, the lectern, the Penn pennants and armour hanging from the crossing piers and the Edney gates and box pews.* July 1828. Bristol Museums and Art Gallery (M1952)

As the grandest and wealthiest church in Bristol, however, St Mary's has been singled out for this myth. Many church bells did in fact ring out over Bristol. A traveller from Wales described the event and he was so disgusted that he turned away from the city and went back home again.[7]

Although most of the congregation were blissfully unaware of the horrors, St Mary's cannot disassociate itself from the slave trade. Edmund Saunders, for example, a church warden in the early eighteenth century, was a prominent Bristol slave trader. The hapless souls were bought in Africa from African slave traders, torn from their homes and families, to be transported on the dreaded 'middle passage' from Africa to the West Indies to work on the sugar plantations. In the later years they were also taken to America, to the cotton and tobacco plantations of the southern colonies. It is an issue much wider than the history of a single church. Let us agree with the words of Hannah More, an active abolitionist who knew the abolitionists Thomas Clarkson and William Wilberforce and who had connections with St Mary Redcliffe:

> Whene're to Afric's shores I turn my eyes,
> Horrors of deepest, deadliest guilt arise;
> I see, by more than Fancy's mirror shown,
> The burning village and the blazing town:
> See the dire victims torn from social life,
> The shrieking babe, the agonising wife;
> She, wretch forlorn! is dragg'd by hostile hands,
> To distant tyrants sold, in distant lands!

1. CS 2004

2. Smith p122

3. Daniel Defoe: *Tour through England and Wales*

4. Ibid

5. CS 1975

6. BRO P/StMR/OP/10

7. Dresser and Giles: *Bristol and Transatlantic Slavery* p95

CHAPTER EIGHT

The Poets

Throughout the seventeenth and eighteenth centuries we get scattered snippets of information about the Elizabethan parish school. There were twelve school governors; in 1619 these were Thomas Syssell, John Witherly, William White, George Davis, John Syssell, William Morgan, Richard Burges, William Browne, Thomas Parker, John Yeamans and Thomas Grafton. All twelve were inhabitants of the parish. We discover that in about 1600 the schoolmaster had a stipend of four pounds a year, but John Whitson who died in 1603 left a will in which he bequeathed certain rents, three bushels and a half of wheat and three bushels of rye every year 'for the maintenance and preferment of the schoolmaster of the free school at or neare Redcliffe church...he being an honest and learned scholar and endeavouring to sett forwards poor freemen's children...in the English and Latin tongues.'

We know the names of some of the seventeenth-century schoolmasters. Hugh Roberts held the post in 1662, Robert Mayor in 1666 and Abraham Nicholson in 1669. On 30 November 1682 Tobias Higgins was appointed schoolmaster 'in consideration of the more than ordinary charge that Tobias Higgins, bachelor of arts and citizen of Bristol hath been at repairing and amending the same school and also for the love and affection which they do bear towards him'.

In the eighteenth century we find that Thomas Harris became master of the free school. He seems to have been highly thought of and he was described as 'tory, quiet and good'. He was paid twenty pounds per annum but for this he was expected to spend half his time on church duties, including prayers for Mr Colston, and also some of the duties at All Saints – but this gave him an extra income of seven pounds per annum. His appointment was made in 1731 but a generation later he was not so well thought of and on 6 May 1758 an advertisement appeared for a master to replace Thomas Harris. He was removed 'because he hath not attended the care of the school which is fallen into great decay'. On 8 January 1759 the Rev. Mr Hayward was appointed to replace him.

By the middle of the eighteenth century the Queen Elizabeth Grammar School at Redcliffe had been joined by another educational establishment located a very short distance away. This was the Pile Street Charity School founded to help with the education of the poorer families in the parish. Strict rules were drawn up for the pupils and these rules tell us a great deal about the school and about eighteenth-century schools in general.

The times of attendance varied with the seasons. Thus from 25 March to 29 September school was held from eight in the morning and from two in the afternoon. The finishing times are not given. From 30 September to 24 March the times were nine in the morning and one in the afternoon. Parents were told not to keep the children home on any pretext whatsoever except sickness. An undated hand-written list is given in the school records. Other rules, aimed at both children and parents, were:

> That they [the parents] send them [the children] clean washed and combed.
>
> That they keep their clothing, stockings and shoes in good repair and that the boys are not to have their second best coat till the first day of the September Fair following and that the boys do always ware their Red Stockings in and out of school.
>
> That they set their children good examples and keep them in good order at home, obliging them to say their prayers morning and evening and to repeat their Catechism and read the Scriptures especially on the Lords Day.
>
> That they conduct themselves properly in all places and at all times particularly to their parents and master or benefactor and also to behave to all persons with becoming respect.
>
> That they are not to be seen in the street after 8 o'clock in the evening unless on some proper errand.
>
> No boy to be admitted whose brother has been expelled this school unless the conduct of the parents as well as the child be approved by the gentlemen at the quarterly meeting which conduct may be inspected by the master or some other person.
>
> Impertinence shewne to any of the subscribers or to the masters of the school will be deemed as an insult to the subscribers at large and will subject the child of the offender to expulsion.
>
> Lastly the parents and children as shall notoriously break through these rules will be excluded all benefit of this charity.

[But this was not the last rule. There were still a few afterthoughts to come.]

Clothes worn on Sunday to be returned to the master every Monday morning in proper condition.

They are to appear at school with a clean band and shirt on Sundays and Thursdays and on Tuesdays and Saturdays with a clean band.

All amusements which tend to corrupt the morals or to injure the health are expressly forbidden, a breach of this rule is punished at the master's discretion.

All swearing, lying and suchlike offences are considered as a breach of human divine laws and subjects the offender to severe and certain punishment.

You [dear parents] are to take notice that if your son is seen out without the whole of the charity clothes on [including the bright red stockings] he will be immediately suspended from the school.

By order of the treasurer, E Giles master[1]

At this time there were forty boys in the school and each one was supplied with a coat, waistcoat, breeches and shoes, two bands and two shirts, a pair of stockings and a cap. It was customary for them to be given a spare pair of the bright red school stockings at Christmas.

The school was opened in 1733 and William Wallice was the first master. In 1738 Wallice was succeeded by Thomas Chatterton who continued as master until his death in August 1752. The Chattertons had been associated with St Mary's for at least two generations, some as stonecutters and another branch of the family as sextons. On 20 November in the year that Thomas Chatterton died a posthumous child was born in the schoolhouse at Pile Street. The boy was named after his father.

The younger Thomas Chatterton's early life and education was at Pile Street where he wore the red stockings and the white shoulder band of the Charity School. He was an able pupil and when he was older his mother was able to send him on to Colston's School to further his education. Colston's School at this time was housed in a rambling Tudor building that had originally been one of the Bristol Friaries. On leaving school at the age of fourteen the young Chatterton was apprenticed to an attorney called John Lambert. It is frequently assumed that his job with Lambert and his connections with the church gave him access to the church records and that by this means he

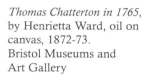

Thomas Chatterton in 1765, by Henrietta Ward, oil on canvas, 1872-73. Bristol Museums and Art Gallery

worked hard at reading the early manuscripts, learning something of the history of the church. This is not quite the whole story. It seems that before young Thomas was born the boy's father managed to get hold of a large quantity of old documents from the parish chest. These priceless records of early church history were seen as of no value whatever, so Thomas Chatterton senior decided to keep them for himself to be used as scribbling paper and wrapping paper for his family. This surely is the reason for the missing documents from the early centuries of St Mary Redcliffe. The church records from the Middle Ages were used to wrap parcels. Accounts of the damage caused by the fifteenth-century fall of the spire were used as children's scribbling pads. Priceless records from earlier times were used to wrap up the scraps from the kitchen and to kindle the fire. Who was at fault? Certainly not the young Thomas Chatterton. Was it the fault of his father? Surely the parish clerk, or somebody senior in the church should have prevented this disaster, yet nobody seemed to care. The dusty ancient parchments were seen as being of no value.

The documents must have remained in the household until Chatterton reached his teens for he became very interested in the old vocabulary and the medieval style of writing and he began to decipher them. He read and copied them and he taught himself to write with the same antiquated style and spellings. Chatterton's history of St

Mary Redcliffe is seen as mainly fiction but the fact is that he may well have uncovered things about the history of St Mary Redcliffe which can no longer be discovered.

In 1768 there was a major event in Bristol. The old Bristol Bridge, built five centuries earlier in the thirteenth century to replace the even older Saxon Bridge, was no longer able to carry the great volume of traffic in England's second city. The quaint houses and the chapel on the bridge were torn down to build a more efficient but nondescript new bridge and to satisfy the needs of the traffic. When the new bridge was opened the newspaper *Felix Farley s Bristol Journal* received a beautiful piece of poetry from Chatterton referring to the building of the previous Bristol Bridge 500 years earlier:

> Now agayne with bremie Force,
> Severn in his auntient Course,
> Rolls his rappyd streeme alonge,
> With a Sable, swift and stronge
> Movynge manie a okie wode-
> We, the Menne of Brystowe towne,
> Have yreed this Brydge of Stone;
> Wyshynge echome it maie last,
> Till the date of daies be past
> Standynge where the other stode

The antiquarians were fascinated. The poetry must be older than Chaucer, more than a century earlier than Langland. It had wonderful rhythm and strength, a truly remarkable discovery of English verse from the thirteenth century. The author hid under the pseudonym of 'Dunhelmus Bristoliensuis' but the public clamoured to know more about the antiquarian who had found this remarkable work.

What they discovered was quite amazing. The name of the person who had submitted the verse was Thomas Chatterton. Nobody doubted the authenticity of the account. Had they known the truth, that Chatterton had actually written the account and the poetry himself, they would have been speechless with disbelief.

To the delight of the antiquarians Chatterton produced more fascinating manuscripts relating to old Bristol. They seemed very authentic because he was able to use the style and wording of the old manuscripts from the Redcliffe parish chest. Two pewter merchants, George Catcot and Henry Burgum, befriended the boy. Catcot was something of an eccentric who climbed a church steeple for a bet and kept a box with a label 'My teeth to be put in the coffin when I die'. His partner Burgum was anxious to prove his family pedigree and he was delighted when the adolescent Chatterton produced a coat of arms for the de Burgum family – the honest pewterer suspected nothing when he found that his family coat of arms contained three golden hippopotami! Chatterton's forgeries were very convincing and he went on to produce some wonderful medieval poetry which he claimed was written by a fifteenth-century monk called Thomas Rowley but which he had written in the same style as the Bristol Bridge poem.

   The deception could not last, Thomas Chatterton knew that he had a talent but he desperately needed a wealthy patron to publish his work. The Bristol people were beginning to get suspicious, they asked him too many questions about his discoveries and his sources, and in the spring of 1770 he terminated his apprenticeship to John Lambert and left home to try his fortune in London. He wrote to Horace Walpole, a patron of the arts, hoping to obtain sponsorship. His letters home were happy and cheerful and he found that he loved the freedom of the capital city after his provincial life. One of his letters shows that his adolescent interest in the fair sex was aroused before he left Bristol:

> My sister will remember me to Miss Sandford. I have not quite forgot her; though there are so many pretty milliners &c. that I have quite forgot myself – Miss Rumsey, if she comes to London, would do well as an old acquaintance to send me her address. London is not Bristol – we may patrol the town for a day, without raising one whisper or nod of scandal. If she refuses may the curse of all antiquated virgins fall on her...[2]

Chatterton tried his hand at political satire and at first he seemed to make good contacts. He was unlucky however, in that his contacts ran into business problems and his income suffered accordingly. Horace Walpole replied to his request for sponsorship but he did not offer any money. Chatterton's income began to dry up and his mood fluctuated between optimism and depression. His poetic temperament was extremely

Left: Sculptor Laurence Holofcener's *Thomas Chatterton* on Millennium Square, Bristol.

Below: The iron-bound wooden chest once held the parish documents which, reputedly, Chatterton used as inspiration for his writing.

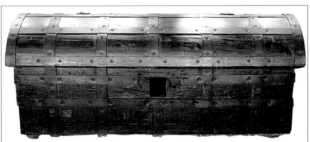

sensitive and this, coupled with the strong emotions of puberty, accounted for his drastic swings of mood. On 25 August 1770 Thomas Chatterton's mood reached rock bottom. He took arsenic and died in his attic room at Holborn.

Recent research has shown that Chatterton may not in fact have committed suicide. He certainly died of arsenic poisoning but we now know that he was taking arsenic as a medicine because he had developed syphilis. At this distance in time the question can probably never be fully resolved.

Following Chatterton's death the controversy continued over the authenticity of his

Rowley Poems. When the famous Doctor Samuel Johnson visited Bristol in 1776 he was persuaded to go to St Mary Redcliffe to try and settle this controversy. Catcot was convinced that if the sceptical Doctor Samuel Johnson could but see the chest where Chatterton found his manuscripts then the learned doctor would become a convert. In fact most of Chatterton's information probably came from the throw-away manuscripts which his father had collected, but the tradition that he was allowed access to the parish chest probably holds some truth. Johnson's biographer James Boswell described the incident in graphic detail and is worth quoting at length:

> George Catcot, the pewterer, who was as zealous for Rowley, as Dr Hugh Blair was for Ossian (I trust my Reverend friend will excuse the comparison), attended us at our inn, and with a triumphant air of lively simplicity called out, 'I'll make Dr. Johnson a convert.' Dr. Johnson, at his desire, read aloud some of Chatterton's fabricated verses, while Catcot stood at the back of his chair, moving himself like a pendulum, and beating time with his feet, and now and then looking into Dr. Johnson's face, wondering that he was not yet convinced. We called on Mr. Barret, the surgeon, and saw some of the originals as they were called, which were executed very artificially; but from a careful inspection of them, and a consideration of the circumstances with which they were attended we were quite satisfied of the imposture, which, indeed, has been clearly demonstrated from internal evidence, by several able criticks.
>
> Honest Catcot seemed to pay no attention what ever to any objections, but insisted, as an end to all controversy, that we should go with him to the tower of the church of St Mary, Redcliffe, and *view with our own eyes* the ancient chest in which the manuscripts were found. To this, Dr. Johnson good-naturedly agreed; and though troubled with a shortness of breathing, laboured up a long flight of steps, till we came to the place where the wonderous chest stood. '*There*, (said Catcot with a bouncing confident credulity,) *there* is the very chest itself.' After this *ocular demonstration*, there was no more to be said. He brought to my recollection a Scotch Highlander, a man of learning too, and who had seen the world, attesting, and at the same time giving his reasons for the authenticity of Fingal: 'I have heard all that poem when I was young.' – 'Have you, Sir? Pray what have you heard?' 'I have heard Ossian, Oscar, and *every one of them*.'

Johnson said of Chatterton, 'This is the most extraordinary young man that has encountered my knowledge. It is wonderful how the whelp has written such things.' We were by no means pleased with our inn at Bristol. 'Let us see now, (said I,) how we should describe it.' Johnson was ready with his raillery. 'Describe it, Sir? – Why, it was so bad that Boswell wished to be in Scotland!'[3]

The introduction of Samuel Johnson brings us to the involvement of Hannah More. Hannah, like Thomas Chatterton, was born in a schoolhouse. In her case, in the rural village of Stapleton about seven years before Chatterton was born. Sarah Chatterton, mother of Thomas, was also from Stapleton and the two women were good friends. When Sarah Chatterton was struggling as a single mother to bring up her children Hannah helped with the expenses and on one occasion she raised the sum of thirty pounds to help the Chattertons. Hannah More was a great friend of Samuel Johnson and on her visits to London she was a regular member of his circle. She tells us in her own words how Samuel Johnson ragged her about her involvement with Thomas Chatterton:

One of the company happened to say a word about poetry. 'Hush hush' said he, 'it is dangerous to say a work of poetry before her'. He continued to joke and lamented that I had not married Chatterton, that posterity might have seen a propagation of poets.[4]

Samuel Johnson's opinion dealt Chatterton a serious blow. The Bristol historians soon discovered Chatterton's attempts to falsify the history of their city and they had no sympathy with him. His works actually included a history of St Mary Redcliffe but this has been discredited along with the rest of his historical works. And yet his inspiration and his data came from church records that we can no longer see and read. There will always remain an uneasy feeling that perhaps some of Chatterton's history is correct but we do not know which parts to believe and which to discredit.

Others depicted Thomas Chatterton as the poor poet striving for recognition who had taken his own life in despair. But we cannot close the story of Thomas Chatterton at this point. After his death his work was published and became better known. His suicide became a fascination for artists and writers. In 1790 John Flaxman painted the spirit of despair giving the cup of poison to Chatterton, in 1794 Edward Orme painted his famous picture of his death scene, the Frenchman Foreau's picture appeared in 1842 and Henry Wallis' famous death-bed scene, now housed at Tate Britain, was painted in 1856. The playwrights were equally fascinated by the tragedy. Alfred de Vigny's play *Chatterton* opened at the Theatre Français in 1835 and later in the century Leoncavallo dedicated an opera to the boy poet.

It was in the generation after Chatterton that the Romantic poets came to the fore, and Bristol had a part to play in this movement. Robert Southey was born in Wine Street Bristol in 1774. He befriended Coleridge who was two years his junior and William Wordsworth who was born in 1770, the year that Chatterton died. These three wandered around Bristol and its surrounds and they were fascinated by the story of the boy poet. They cared little for his historical falsifications but they loved his poetry and they felt that he was an inspiration to all of them.

Chatterton was one of the reasons why both Southey and Coleridge were drawn to St Mary Redcliffe. The other reasons were two sisters Sarah and Edith Fricker who lived in the parish. Both the poets were married at St Mary Redcliffe within a month of each other in the year 1795, both by the vicar Benjamin Spry. The brides' father was a sugar-mould maker at Westbury-on-Trym and their mother had been a school-mistress. It seemed on the face of it a very glamorous double wedding but Southey's licence fee was paid by his publisher Cottle as was the wedding ring. We do not know what passed through the mind of Mrs Fricker as she saw both her daughters committing themselves to marry poets, especially when the penniless Southey took leave of his new wife as soon as he reached the church door to undertake a long trip to Portugal. As for Coleridge, he was persuaded by his friend Southey that he was under an obligation to marry Sarah Fricker because she had been refusing advances from other men on his behalf.

Coleridge moved to Keswick to be near his friend William Wordsworth and often, as they roamed the Lakeland fells or, back in the West Country, the Quantocks trying out new ideas on each other, they would discuss Thomas Chatterton. They had access to his works, in fact Southey worked on the first edition of Chatterton's poems so they all had a very good ideas of the boy's talent. All three poets wrote something about Chatterton. Southey put his feelings into verse:

The Chatterton Memorial by S C Fripp at the north porch, erected in 1839 but subsequently dismantled.

O Chatterton! That thou wert yet alive!

Sure thou woulds't spread the canvass to the gale,

And love with us the tinkling team to drive

O'er peaceful Freedom's undivided dale.

Coleridge was in complete agreement:

Flower that must perish! shall I liken thee

To some sweet girl of too too rapid growth

Nipped by consumption mid untimely charms?

Or to Bristowa's bard, the wondrous boy!

An amaranth, which earth scarce seemed to own,

Till disappointment came, and pelting wrong

Beat it to earth…

Wordsworth felt that Chatterton had a claim to be the first of the Romantic poets. The marvellous natural grasp of words and metre coming from so young a person was quite amazing; none of the later poets had achieved the same degree of authority at so young an age. William Wordsworth used his poetic licence when he had Chatterton following his plough on the mountainside – how he would love to have shown the boy his lakeland scenery. His sentiments echo those of his two friends:

I thought of Chatterton, the marvellous Boy,

The sleepless Soul that perished with his pride;

Of him who walked in glory and in joy

Following his plough, along the mountain-side:

By our own spirits we are deified:

We Poets in our youth begin in gladness;

But there of come in the end despondency and madness.

We quote from Southey, Coleridge and Wordsworth. Yet ask anybody in Bristol to quote from Chatterton and we are very unlikely to get anything for an answer. His life was so short that his poetic output was minimal compared to his successors. He wrote

The Bristowe Tragedy, Onn Oure Ladies Chyrch and *An Excelente Balade of Charitie*. To redress the balance two little verses are given from Chatterton's *Song of Ella* which he also called *A Tragycall Enterlude*. Here he writes of a girl grieving for a lover who had died – the dead lover could well be Chatterton himself.

Song From Ella

O sing unto my roundelay,

O drop the briny tear with me;

Dance no more at holyday,

Like a running river be:

My love is dead,

Gone to his death-bed

All under the willow-tree.

Come, with acorn cup and thorn,

Drain my heartes blood away

Life and all its good I scorn,

Dance by night, or fest by day

My love is dead,

Gone to his death-bed

All under the willow-tree.

1. BRO P/St MR/Sch/2(b)

2. John Cranstone Nevill: *Thomas Chatterton* (1948)

3. James Boswell: *The Life of Samuel Johnson*

4. Anne Stott: *Hannah More, The first Victorian*

CHAPTER NINE

The Crowning Glory

In the first years of the nineteenth century school holidays were granted to celebrate religious festivals, state events and royal occasions. The anniversary of the execution of Charles I and the restoration of the monarchy were always a holiday for the children, as was the anniversary of the gunpowder plot on 5 November. Sometimes the holiday was a full day but usually only half a day was given:

School Holidays, St Mary Redcliffe Parish School, Reign of King George III

21 Dec to 2 Jan	Christmas	
18 Jan	The Queen's Birthday	½ day
30 Jan	King Charles Martyrdom	½ day
Shrove Tuesday out at 11 o'clock		
Ash Wednesday		½ day
14 Feb	Valentine's day	½ day
Every epistle and gospel day which falls		
on Tuesday or Thursday		½ day
Thursday before Easter to 'the Monday after Easter week'		
29 May	King Charles' Restoration	½ day
Holy Thursday		½ day
4 June	King's birthday	1 day
24 June	Midsummer day	1 day
At March and September fair		1 day
22 Sep	King's coronation	1 day
29 Sep	Michaelmas day	½ day
5 Nov	Gunpowder plot	½ day
13 Nov	Colston's birthday	1 day
Also any public rejoicing …[1]		

Education for girls first came to the parish when the charity school for girls opened on Redcliffe Hill in 1793 and the school remained in existence until 1884 by which time a larger and better school for girls was well established in Redcliffe Parade.

Some idea of the degree of literacy in Redcliffe Parish can be obtained from the charity school records in the first decade of the nineteenth century. Every parent was given clothing to the value of twenty pounds, each one had to sign to say that if they did not return the clothing when the boy left school they were required to pay the school treasurer the twenty pounds. This was a lot of money; a generation later

St Mary Redcliffe from the East, 1831. William Muller's watercolour shows the east end of the church with the pond in the foreground.

Dickens's clerk Bob Cratchet earned a mere ten shillings per week. In 1808 there were fifteen signatures and twenty crosses – literacy of 43% for this small sample.

In the early nineteenth century the area around Redcliffe was a curious mixture of rural and industrial development. This was a prime period for the Bristol School of Artists (as they many years later came to be described) and many of them chose to illustrate the scenes in Redcliffe. Thus T L Rowbotham's view from the northeast of the church shows a cockerel perched on a farm trailer with a few hens scratching around a farmyard. He shows a small pond and a large water barrel with a pair of

Nicholas Pocock, *St Mary Redcliffe from Sea Banks*, etching, aquatint and watercolour, circa 1782.
Bristol Museums and Art Gallery (Mb5089)

Thomas Girtin, *Bristol Harbour*, pencil and watercolour, 1800. Bristol Museums and Art Gallery (K532)

Top: John Sell Cotman, *St Mary Redcliffe, Bristol, Dawn,* circa 1802, watercolour. The Trustees of the British Museum 1859-529-117.
Bottom: George Holmes, *Wharfside activity,* circa 1810. The view is from Welsh Back.

James Johnson, *Redcliffe Street*, circa 1821, oil on canvas. Bristol Museums and Art Gallery (K2828)

Thomas L Rowbotham, *St Mary Redcliffe and the Shot Tower with Droitwich Patent Salt Co. seen from the Ferry Slip*, 1826. Bristol Museums and Art Gallery (M2936)

Samuel Jackson, *St Mary Redcliffe and Redcliffe Parade from Prince Street Bridge*, 1825, watercolour. Bristol Museums and Art Gallery (M2927)

William James Muller, *The Bristol Riots; burning of the toll-houses on Prince Street Bridge with St Mary Redcliffe,* oil on paper, 1831. Bristol Museums and Art Gallery (M4108)

Joseph Walter, *The Floating Harbour with Prince Street Bridge and St Mary Redcliffe,* oil on canvas, 1842. Bristol Museums and Art Gallery (K1178)

Lithograph by Hullmandel and Walton dedicated to *Nil Desperandum* (Thomas Proctor), *The choir from the nave,* circa 1850. Bristol Museums and Art Gallery (M720)

Tristram Hillier RA, *The Inner Pool, Bristol*, 1960, oil on canvas. Bristol Museums and Art Gallery (K2919)

James Johnson, *The nave of St Mary Redcliffe with the centre panel of the Hogarth altarpiece,* 1828, watercolour. Bristol Museums and Art Gallery (M1949)

James Johnson, *Interior of the outer north porch from the inner porch*, 1828, watercolour.
Bristol Museums and Art Gallery (M1946)

T L Rowbotham, *The towers of St Mary Redcliffe and the shot manufactory seen from Redcliffe Back*, pencil and watercolour, 1828. Bristol Museums and Art Gallery (M1933)

wheels and shafts. Some of the Pile Street houses are shown with washing hanging out to dry. The same artist also painted the church from a point outside the north transept showing a similar rooster chaperoning four hens; he shows also a horse with its cart housed in a farm shed. The farm buildings appear to be built directly onto the wall of the church. William Muller painted a rural scene from a point close to Rowbotham's view showing a wonderful skyscape, a large pond and a huddle of sheep with more of their flock grazing in the distance. St Mary Redcliffe has become a grand idyllic country church standing serenely over a timeless English scene. George Delamotte in 1825 shows Pump Street running past the east end of the church on the left, looking down a rural lane with a row of country cottages and farm buildings to the right.

James Johnson's view from the north is much more urban than rural and it shows the church tower presiding over a busy Redcliffe full of street life and action. There are pubs, gabled houses and shop fronts. It is populated by a street musician, a mother carrying a child, a boy with a hoop, a man carrying milk or water and a woman holding a basket on her head. There is a horse, a donkey and a small dog. Another view shows the upper stretch of Redcliffe Hill where the ugly shot tower, with the advantage of the hill, competed with the church spire for the tallest building on the

A lively view of the church, with the traffic on Redcliffe Hill in Regency times. Lithograph circa 1830.

skyline. The shot tower was symbolic of an important Redcliffe industry. The plumber William Watts perfected the technique whereby droplets of molten lead fell from the top of the tower under gravity and formed perfect spherical balls when they solidified and hit the water at the bottom. The method was so successful that William Watts became wealthy enough to embark on building Windsor Terrace in Clifton out of his profits, but the enterprise bankrupted him.

Pottery and glass were well established at this time and were major forms of employment. The apprentice records surviving from the period indicate other more traditional forms of employment. In 1826 John Pike was apprenticed to Thomas Lucas, a pastry cook, and his wife Jemima. He was paid only four shillings a week, with a rise of one shilling a week every year for seven years until he had completed his apprenticeship. He was better paid than Richard Skidmore who was apprenticed to Walter and Hannah Wilmot as a glasscutter. Young Skidmore received only two shillings a week in his first year, followed by the same annual increase of one shilling per week. In 1829 Sam Barnes was apprenticed as a cordwainer to George Watts and his wife Elizabeth. In the same year Edward Pyke was apprenticed as a hairdresser to William Salmon

Photograph, looking over the Floating Harbour from the newly completed spire of St Mary Redcliffe, 1872. Bristol Museums and Art Gallery (Ma4151)

Howard and Joseph Clark was apprenticed to William Cook, a sailmaker. All the apprentices received a similar low salary of a few shillings per week, but after seven years all were qualified with a trade with which to earn their livelihood.[2]

In 1831 a company of actors arrived in Bristol to play at the Theatre Royal in King Street. Among their number was Miss Fanny Kemble, the niece of Sarah Siddons and the daughter of Phillip Kemble who was also one of the travelling company. Fanny kept a very lively journal which gives us fascinating information about the backstage panics at the theatre, but on Sundays she went to church with her father and with her

chaperone, Dall. On 10 July they decided to go to the service at the cathedral. 'My father wickedly dawdled about till we were late and we had to scamper along the quays and steep streets,' she complained. But her main grievance was that she had to suffer 'a wretchedly poor sermon'. It may be a mere coincidence, but this was the very year in which the preacher Sydney Smith gave his notorious sermons in Bristol Cathedral, so controversial that the Mayor and the corporation left to attend St Mary Redcliffe. Fanny and her little party followed suit.[3]

The following Sunday, 17 July, the little group decided to go to the morning service at St Mary Redcliffe instead. The Rev. Martin Whish was vicar at the time, and holds the distinction of serving in the capacity of vicar for 46 years, longer than any other incumbent. Fanny was complimentary about the church architecture but we discover that the sermon was not a great improvement on the previous Sunday:

> To Redcliffe church with my father and Dall. What a beautiful old building it is! …
> What a sermon! Has the truth, as our church holds it, no fitter expounders than
> such a preacher? Are these its stays, props, pillars – teachers to guide, enlighten, and

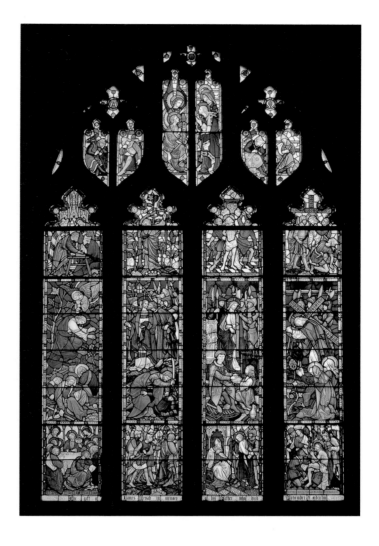

The Passion Window at the east end of the south ambulatory is one of the finest surviving examples of Victorian glass in the church. It was commissioned from Clayton and Bell in 1861.

Opposite: T L Rowbotham, *St Mary Redcliffe from the East*, April 1826, pencil and watercolour. Bristol Museums and Art Gallery (M1937)

instruct people as cultivated and intelligent as the people of this country on the most momentous of all subjects? Are these the sort of adversaries to oppose men like Channing? As for not going to church because of bad or foolish sermons that is another matter, though I not infrequently hear that reason assigned for staying away. One goes to church to say ones prayers, and not to hear more or less fine discourses; one goes because it is ones duty, and a delight and comfort, and a quite distinct duty and delight from that of private prayer. A good sermon, heaven knows, is a rare blessing to be thankful for, but if one went to church only in the expectation of that blessing, one might stay away most Sundays in the year. [4]

It was in the 1840s that the first photographs began to appear. They are crude and

Victorian photographs show what centuries of unfettered air pollution had done to the fabric of the church, a reality that artists had chosen to ignore.

unfocussed, the contrast is harsh with no shades of grey between the black and white but they are valuable and truthful images of the times. The first photographs of St Mary Redcliffe show that the painters of the Regency age used a lot of artistic licence in the depictions of their clean and beautiful church. The photographs show a shocking state of decay in the church fabric where, after centuries of unmonitored pollution from the Redcliffe industries, the walls and the carvings all over the outside of the church were encrusted in soot. On both north and south porch the dirt was engrained into the stonework and there were ugly fungal growths around windows and buttresses. The church was situated next door to the largest glass cone in Bristol and the deposits from years of low-quality smoky coal had taken their toll on the church fabric. It was no wonder that in 1842 a restoration committee was launched with an appeal for the sum of forty thous-and pounds to clean up the church. Six years later the Canynges Society was formed to help raise the money. It was a gargantuan

Britton's plan shows the
layout of the church in 1842.
Note the roof vaulting
patterns at the east and west
end of the church and also
in the two porches.

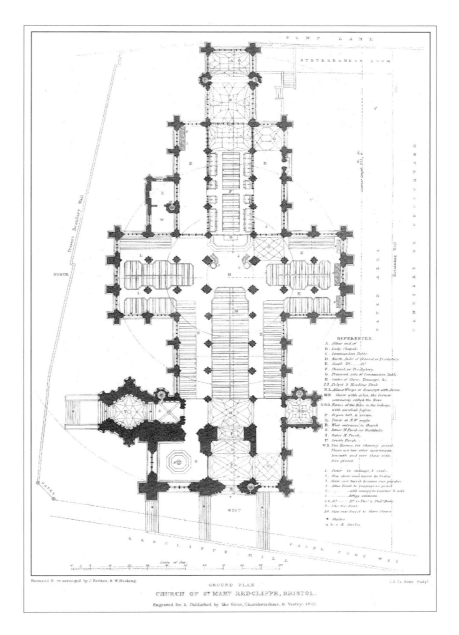

task but for decades the public of Bristol were exhorted to give towards the restoration fund. The rustic houses depicted by the artists, which abutted on the north side of the church grounds, were removed at this time and in 1851 a model of the church was on show at Prince Albert's Great Exhibition in Hyde Park – no doubt with a view to giving the church a national profile and in the hope of finding more sponsors nationally.

In the 1850s came the closure of the Elizabethan school which had been housed in

With and without the Harris and Byfield organ: the right-hand photograph from sometime after 1857.

the Lady Chapel for about 100 years. The school had been on the decline since the early decades of the century through lack of funds. Edward Parsons, the master of the school, resigned in 1830 and from that time onwards nobody could be recruited to fill the post. The school was therefore effectively closed from 1830, but it was theoretically still solvent for another twenty years during which time there was not a single governors' meeting. Official closure came in 1854 and three years later the wall was removed so that the Lady Chapel could be used again for its original function.

The Pile Street Charity School also closed at about the same time. Canon George Madan, the vicar at the time, generously allowed part of the extensive vicarage garden to be used for a new school. The school was in Redcliffe Parade. It marked a great step forward when it was opened in 1855 because it accommodated both sexes, girls on the upper floor, boys on the ground floor. The new school was the ancestor of what became St Mary Redcliffe School.

The main fundraising efforts in the 1850s were directed towards the church fabric, but an exception was made in 1856 when a new pulpit was installed. It was a very fine piece of carving by the Quaker William Bennett. Around the pulpit were carved effigies of the twelve apostles each holding a symbol by which they could be identified. Bennett loved to carve his figures from live models and the twelve apostles were his Quaker friends. He also chose to include angels with his carvings and to this end he dressed his daughters in white sheets to model for him. Many years later his great-granddaughter confirmed this story. It is also thought that the elaborate carvings on the pew ends in the nave and aisles are the work of William Bennett.

The fundraising to restore the church continued unceasingly. Good progress was made but it was slow work. The restoration had been underway for ten

The Victorian pulpit installed in 1856 and created by William Bennett, a Quaker who liked to carve from live models such as friends and family.

years, but the ten years turned into twenty and the job was still far from finished. The Victorians had made up their minds that St Mary Redcliffe's crowning glory, the spire that had fallen so long ago in the fifteenth century, was to be rebuilt with the advantage of lightning conductors and modern technology. The scaffolding, which had enclosed the walls for restoration, surrounded the tower and the new spire. Parishioners looked on with wonder as stone by stone the spire grew slowly taller and taller. It was wonderful and very moving to see the spire returning again after so many years. At long last, thirty years after the formation of the restoration fund, the spire was almost complete. Only the capstone and the weather vane still had to be fitted. This surely was a great day in the history of the ancient church by the Red Cliff. It was agreed to celebrate the occasion by having a ceremonial laying of the capstone. The date fixed was Thursday, 11 May 1872.

It was a red letter day for the people of Redcliffe and for the whole of Bristol.

When the spire was restored in the nineteenth century medieval scaffolding techniques were used. The placing of the capstone on the completed spire was celebrated across all of Bristol.

Crowds gathered in Redcliffe Street, Phippin Street and all the neighbouring streets where there was a good view of the church. Every available window was packed with people waving flags and bunting, many had scrambled through the skylights and sat on the roofs of their houses. There was a carnival atmosphere. The event was scheduled to start at two o'clock and the excitement rose as his worship the mayor, Mr Proctor Baker, and his wife arrived punctually at the church to perform the ceremony.

Then came a bad omen. A sudden heavy shower of rain came on, there were flashes of lightning and peals of thunder. Was it not a thunderstorm which had brought down the spire 400 years ago? The mayor and mayoress took shelter inside the church and the great crowd did the best they could to avoid a drenching. The mayor and his wife re-emerged about half an hour later when the storm had blown over. Then the action began:

The mayoress displayed a surprising amount of firmness, and although his worship [the mayor] appeared quite cool, his better half had evidently the best of him, in that respect. As soon as the hoist began to move the vast crowd commenced cheering heartily, and the mayor took off his hat and bowed his acknowledgements. The cheering continued all the time the hoist was slowly rising, and its occupants were safely landed on the first stage, a height of 160 feet above the level of the hill. From this point to the summit of the tower the usual ascent is by means of ladders, but a special contrivance had been brought into requisition for the occasion. This consisted of a second hoist, worked by hand. It was merely two square boards, one overhead and the other underfoot, like the top and bottom of a box, with a rope at each corner, covered on three sides with drapery. Into this the mayoress got, and was hoisted by the workmen to the top of the spire. Workmen were stationed at different points to prevent it from swinging too much. His worship however, showed his pluck and disdain of the arrangement by boldly mounting the ladders and he was not long in reaching the top.[5]

They were accompanied by Mr W Rice, clerk of the works. This was only the first of several ascents to the dizzy heights of the spire. The next party to be hoisted up was the vicar, the Reverend Canon Randall with his churchwardens Messrs C B Hare and Mervyn King. Then came a third party, the Reverend Auchmuty the curate, and Mr Edmund King. The Rev. Anstey and Mr A Baker were already at the top waiting to receive the rest of the party. The crowd cheered from their hearts as those at the dizzy height of the spire waved their acknowledgements to those below. The mayoress was not to be outdone by her husband's stunt of climbing up the workmen's ladder. She entertained the crowd below in her own inimitable style:

> The whole party then, one by one, stood upon the capstone, and took a view of the surrounding scenery until the rain began to descent rather heavily when it was deemed desirable to commence the return journey. The mayoress skipped along the planks and about the scaffolding with as much composure as if she had been walking about her own drawing room, and she never betrayed the slightest symptom of fear or misgiving.[6]

The day was one of the most moving in the whole history of the church. Many must have wondered and thought about the fact that this was not the first time a capstone had been set on top of the spire. How we would love to have a record of that day, long long ago and five centuries away even in Victorian times, when the humble parishioners of the fourteenth century celebrated the completion of their beautiful Gothic church which we all know and appreciate so much. It was they, and not the Victorians, who created the church. But the Victorians had played their part. All signs of stuffy Victoriana had gone for the day, the people showed great joy and humour. In the Bristol Record Office is an anonymous and humorous postcard written after the event.

The mayor and the vicar ascended the spire

Lifted up to the capstone they could not mount higher.

'More money we want,' cried the mayor like a hero

'Amen' said the vicar 'Dum spiro spero'.

This means that our colours we've nailed to the mast

We'll restore and we'll beg while our breath it shall last.

If results are but slow our pluck you'll admire

We have faith to succeed for we've finished our spire.

Anon.[7]

The author added a little postscript. He wished that the old cock of theirs had got to the top of the perch and crowed Excelsior.

1. BRO P/St MR/Sch/2(b)

2. BRO P/St MR/OP/3(a to e)

3. Bettey, J (Ed): *Historic Churches and Church Life in Bristol*, B & G Archaeological Soc 2001

4. FA Kemble: *Record of a Girlhood* (1878)

5. BRO P/St MR/ChW/7/6

6. Ibid

7. Ibid

CHAPTER TEN

High Victoriana

In the nineteenth century the coming of the railway soon affected every person in the country. There were immense benefits to be gained from the greatly improved transport system but there was a price to pay and in Bristol it was Temple parish that suffered more than most. The Temple Meadows down by the waters of the Avon was the place where Isambard Brunel built his terminus to the Great Western Railway and it became the focal point for all the railways in the region. At first it seemed that St Mary Redcliffe had escaped lightly from the railway building euphoria, Redcliffe being very conveniently situated for rail passengers without being torn apart by railway developments. But the situation was short lived. It was obvious that the docks, which had always played a major part in the prosperity of Bristol and Redcliffe, had to be connected to the main railway system. There was only one way to connect the Great Western Railway to the docks at the harbour side and that route took the railway right through the middle of St Mary Redcliffe's churchyard.

There was no stopping the progress of the works. The surveyors came to measure out the ground. Bills were presented to Parliament. Planning permission was granted. Soon the railway navvies arrived with picks and shovels and barrows. It was only a short length of railway from Temple Meads to the harbour but it created far more than the average degree of disruption. Redcliffe Hill was in the way. A tunnel was to be constructed to take the rails to a point near Bathurst Basin and from there to the harbourside. If the tunnel had been dug out the hard way like Box tunnel on the Great Western, with the excavations underground, then the graveyard would not have suffered too much, but it was far quicker and cheaper to use the 'cut and fill' technique whereby the churchyard was opened out into a railway cutting and covered over again afterwards. The burial ground was centuries old, with parishioners from many generations buried there, but many graves had to be dug up and many more were disturbed. A new parochial burial ground was purchased in Bedminster and the remains of the interments were carried off and reburied there. Then houses had to be pulled down, their foundations undermined by the tunnel and the cutting, and one side of Guinea Street was demolished.

The greatest loss was the Queen Anne vicarage where the Rev. Thomas Broughton had (or had not) entertained Handel in the eighteenth century. It was a tragedy to lose the beautiful old vicarage but a new large Victorian vicarage was built and Rev. Henry Goldney Randall became the first vicar to live in it. It was more like a block of flats than a private dwelling. The Rt. Rev. Richard Fox Cartwright gives a description:

> I remember being told that the Victorian House had 22 living and bedrooms. There were 17 bedrooms, all the principal ones had dressing rooms as well. The great hall went straight up through the house to a domed glass roof the same size as the hall. One of the front rooms was the vicar's study, containing an enormous desk and a huge glass-fronted bookcase. These had been left by a former vicar. There was a small chapel attached to the front of the house. In all there were 42 rooms. At the back, opening into the upper yard to the Boy's school, was a squash court given by Walter James. The entrance was from Guinea Street. A pair of large brick pillars stood at the entrance, and a carriage drive swept around a central lawn, with tennis court, to the porticoed front door, which faced south. In the front of the house a large plane tree...[1]

Industry continued to thrive in Redcliffe and Bedminster. The coal industry, which for centuries had been confined to the Kingswood area outside Bristol, expanded to many new locations as further seams of coal were discovered. Redcliffe had no coal, but nearby Bedminster had one of the richest seams in the area and this was first exploited in the nineteenth century. The industry sprouted deep mine shafts, long tunnels to extract the coal from the seams, pit ponies and underground railways, winding gear, slagheaps and coal yards on the surface. The coal was not of the highest quality but it was good household coal. The heating of the homes in southern Bristol generated large quantities of smoke and pollution everywhere.

Many fortunes were made in Victorian times and many self-made men and women became philanthropists and used their wealth to try and ease the sufferings of the poor. An example is Samuel Plimsoll who was born in Redcliffe. He was the eighth of seventeen children. His parents did not frequent the grand church of St Mary's but they attended the Bridge Street Independent Chapel where he was baptised. Young Plimsoll hardly knew anything of Redcliffe for his parents moved to Penrith in

Cumberland when he was four years old. Samuel Plimsoll prospered, however, had a successful parliamentary career and became the Member of Parliament for Derby. In 1873 he returned to his birthplace at Bristol where he was campaigning to improve the conditions of the sailors. He carried a bill through parliament whereby every ship was to carry a Plimsoll Line, a simple device which showed how low the ship lay in the water and which always had to be visible when a ship left port so that she could be seen not to be overloaded.

In 1889 the Rev. C H Awdry, who had been appointed as the diocesan inspector in religious knowledge, produced a report on the Redcliffe schools. At this time there were no fewer than six schools under the jurisdiction of St Mary Redcliffe. The Rev. Awdry wrote of the Endowed Boys' School that 'The result of my examination is sufficient proof of the careful training which these boys continue to receive. The subjects, one and all, have been thoroughly taught, and the way in which the different groups answered reflects the highest credit on the master and his assistants. The tone and order are excellent'. The Girls' School, he wrote, 'continues to be a very prosperous and well ordered school. I was much pleased with the general tone and the ready accurate answers on Holy Scripture and the catechism given by each of the groups, and I was glad to find some elementary knowledge of the order for morning and evening prayer'.

He also described the Blue Girls' School: 'The school is doing well under its new teacher. The tone and order are good. The repetition and written work was correctly done and the children answered readily on the subjects offered'. Writing about the Pile Street Mixed School he reported that 'I still hold the opinion that this school is calculated to do a very useful work in the parish. Those who have been regular in attendance answered simple questions sensibly and well, both in the scriptures and catechism and their repetition of text was good'. There were also two infant schools both of which received his praise. They were the St Mary Redcliffe Infants' School and the Barnard's Place Infants' School. 'All goes on very pleasantly and well in this school. The little ones are in thoroughly good order, and their repetition accurate, and answered simple questions brightly'.

The mention of the Barnard's Place School requires some explanation. In the 1870s St Mary's opened up a mission church in Barnard's Place, situated at the end of Somerset Street at the junction with Clarence Road on the New Cut. The mission had

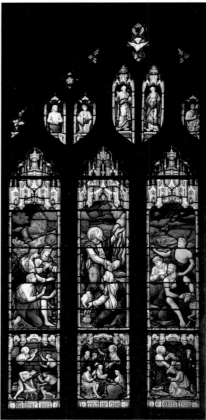

Opposite: The window in the south transept. The top row of lights celebrates Cabot's voyage of 1497. The middle row celebrates the builders and founders of the church. The third row shows famous Bristolians of the fifteenth century: John Jay, William Worcestre, John Carpenter and Thomas Yonge.

Above: The Noah window tells the Old Testament story of Noah's ark. The ark is depicted at the top left, animals appear in the other lights.

Left: The west window was installed in 1868 and paid for by Sholto Hare, a manufacturer of floorcloth. The upper panel depicts Christ in Majesty. The lower panel shows Mary surrounded by scenes from the childhood of Jesus.

several purposes. Firstly it was hoped to
provide services and a Christian community
for the many casual sailors in Bristol, many of
them from foreign parts and sometimes only in
Bristol for a few days. It also provided a
necessary place of worship for some of the
poorer classes in Redcliffe. The grandeur of St
Mary Redcliffe was too intimidating for many
people and it was very difficult to entice them
into a church which they felt was the preserve
of the wealthy. The mission church provided
an alternative, it had its own church rooms and
societies and it also had its infants' school. In
1881 on Sunday 8 October a census was taken
at every church in Bristol to determine the total
numbers attending church, the census showing
clearly the value of the mission church. At St
Mary Redcliffe the attendance figures were 709
at the morning service and 897 at evensong.
The mission church had 196 at the morning
service and 289 in the evening. The total
attendance figure for the whole of Bristol was
given as 45,508.

In the 1880s we have for the first time a
parish magazine to give monthly news on all
the events in the parish. The credit for creating
the magazine must be given primarily to
Charles Edward Cornish who was vicar from
1882 to 1899. In the September edition of 1889
there is an article on the mission church at the
time it was redecorated:

The vestry of the mission church hardly

knows itself, having assumed quite an ecclesiastical appearance. We are extremely grateful to the landlord (the vestry of St Mary Redcliffe) for the pretty and suitable way in which it has been redecorated. It was not before it was required. Worshippers will have noted that a candlestick has been placed in the pulpit. This will enable us to turn down the gas during the sermon. We should have felt the benefit in temperature many Sunday evenings during this summer had we been able to do this besides having prospect of a smaller gas bill.[2]

The magazine describes another drama involving the church spire. It appears that the lightning conductor was found to be faulty and there was a great fear that unless it was repaired very soon the spire was once again at the mercy of a thunderstorm:

> During the past six weeks Redcliffe Spire has been an object of interest to the whole city. It had been discovered that the old lightning conductor was defective. Before it could be removed and a new one substituted for it, it was necessary that someone should ascend to the summit of the spire. This was done in a most bold and daring manner by a steeple jack whose form has since become a familiar one to those who frequent Redcliffe Hill. The last 40 feet he had to ascend without the aid of a rope or ladder. He reached the top by climbing up the ornamented ball flowers which adorn the outside of the spire, and when safely landed on the capstone he fixed a rope and pulley, by which afterwards ladders were raised to their place. This seemed to the churchwardens a favourable opportunity to re-gild and repair the weathercock which has for the last fortnight been deposed from its lofty roosting place.[3]

In the same year Messrs Taylor and Sons of Loughborough repaired the belfry. There were twelve bells. The current peal of bells was completed in 1872 using the bells which had been cast in about 1622. The three heaviest bells weighed only a few pounds less than the three heaviest bells of St Paul's Cathedral in London. In 1877 the latter was considered to be the heaviest ringing peal in the world.

The parish magazines were of a high standard and they provide a wonderful wealth of detail. In 1896 at Bedminster the final of the Bristol School Shields Football was fought. Redcliffe Boys beat Ashton Gate Board school by four goals to two, the result meaning a lot to local prestige.

We discover interesting detail about church services. At Harvest Festival we find that Canon Scobell, the rector of Upton St Leonards, preached from Mark VIII verse 5 with the appropriate text 'How many loaves have ye?' The harvest music was by no means confined to the organ. There were two cornet players, two trombonists and the sound of brass. The sanctuary was decorated with fruit and flowers, bread and vegetables. These were afterwards distributed to 150 needy families in the parish. The seventeenth-century Yeamans' charity was still solvent at this time and deserving families received a loaf of bread every week throughout the year from this charity. The cost of a loaf could be anything from two pence to six pence. The figures for an unspecified year in the nineteenth century were as follows:

Annual gifts:

June 22	Mrs Susanna Compton	16 x 6d loaves	£0	8s 0d
Sep 19	Ann White	80 x 6d loaves	£2	0s 0d
Oct 4	Joseph Bullock	72 x 6d loaves	£1	16s 0d
Nov 5	William James	66 x 2d loaves	£0	11s 0d
Dec 24	Ann Tilley	32 x 6d loaves	£0	16s 0d
Jan 1	Mr Whitchurch	48 x 3d loaves	£0	12s 0d
	Total		£6	3s 0d
8 sixpenny loaves and 23 fourpenny loaves			£0	11s 8d
Given for 52 weeks			£30	6s 8d
Giving a total of			£36	9s 8d[4]

There were plenty of church organisations and social occasions and in the summer there were outings to places of interest. The parish magazine for 1895 describes a men's outing to Weymouth:

A first class saloon had been provided to carry them to Weymouth, which was well filled by a party of more than forty. The start was 5.45 in the pouring rain, but the bad weather was left behind. Weymouth was reached after about four hours, the sky was clear. The only disturbing element was the wind, which proved troublesome on the steamer trip to Portland, by carrying the hats of several unwary passengers into the sea. Arrived at Weymouth the party broke up into groups of three or four and

The first Victorian reredos, installed when Hogarth's altar paintings were thrown out, itself to be replaced in 1871.

did not reassemble until the return journey. All seemed to have enjoyed themselves, some had been for a drive, many had been to Portland and seen the convicts. Some had bought presents for their friends at home. Bristol was reached before eleven again in wet weather but it came too late to spoil the pleasure of the day.[5]

But the more moving and entertaining gatherings were those of the small children. The Christmas tree had been made very popular by Prince Albert and by the 1880s it had become widely accepted throughout the country. The spirit of Christmas was very much alive at the infants' schools. The vicar's wife and the teachers enjoyed the proceedings as much as the children. Several parishioners had given money to be used towards presents for the children and they were invited to be at the gathering to see the children receive them:

> On Monday December the 28th [1885] the Pile Street schoolchildren had their treat in the parish room, in conjunction with Mrs Cornish's mothers meeting and the girls of Miss Hazard's class. After tea the Christmas tree was declared open by Miss Gertrude Anstey, who suddenly appeared out of a large snowball in the room, dressed as Father Christmas, greatly to the amusement of the children.
> After the Christmas tree a large number of prizes were awarded which had been kindly given by the teachers, together with a great quantity given by Mr and Mrs Beloe, Mr and Mrs Colthurst and Miss Bengough, all of whom were present. After a few words of encouragement to the children from the vicar the evening closed, mothers and children being loaded with cake and oranges as they left the room.[6]

There was always the annual summer excursion to the seaside. In 1895 a date at the end of June was chosen and practically all the young children of the parish arrived at Temple Meads in a state of great excitement. As with the men's outing, it was raining but this did nothing to dampen the spirits. Three special trains, each of sixteen carriages, waited at Temple Meads to take over a thousand small children and several hundred parents and helpers to Weston-super-Mare for the annual church outing. Little heads peeped out of the windows. Little noses were pressed to the glass. Little hands waved little handkerchiefs and little voices shouted shrill hurrahs. Excitement mounted as the trains pulled away and after the thrill of the journey the excitement rose even higher when the rain stopped and the trains arrived at the seaside.

Alas. The tide was out.

The children were not dismayed, they doffed their boots and stockings. They dug and played on the beach. The watched the performing dogs, the bagpipes, the sword dancers and the minstrels but most of all they loved the donkey races.[7]

Some of the teachers found their way to the local mission room where they had tea with the Rev. Charles Cornish and his wife who had arrived before them and were ready waiting. At three o'clock silver sixpences were dispensed, one to each child. The coins were very generous gifts for the children to spend as they wished, every child clutched a shining coin tightly in a tiny hand. They ran off to spend them on sweets, souvenirs and donkey rides. Then the scene began to change, Weston became 'super Mare' after all and Ethel Francombe, the daughter of the headmaster of the Endowed Boy's school, described the activity:

> The tide came rolling in, and thousands of little barelegged children were trotting through the curling waves. Oh! What shouts of laughter greeted their funny antics! What careful solicitude on the part of the hundreds of mothers who had joined our excursion and how they enjoyed their freedom![8]

The long summer afternoon changed to evening. It was a very late day for the infants. Darkness was falling on 24 June and they had still not started on their way home. Miss Francombe tells us the happy ending:

> As it grew darker we wended our way back to the train and curled ourselves up in

the corner of a carriage thankful to all the kind friends who by their subscription had helped the little ones to spend one of the happiest days of their lives.[9]

1. *Memories of Redcliffe by Richard Fox Cartwright*, booklet 1993

2. PM 1889

3. PM 1888

4. BRO P/St MR/Ch/10/(b)

5. PM Aug 1895

6. PM Jan 1886

7. PM Aug 1895

8. Ibid

9. Ibid

CHAPTER ELEVEN

Twentieth Century

In the year 1908 when the roof of the church was re-laid the initials of the vicar, the Rev. John Primatt Maud, appeared on the plumber's plate over the south transept. Rev. Maud moved on from his post in 1911 to become the Bishop of Kensington. The vacancy was filled by his son-in-law, the Rev. John Norman Bateman-Champain who married Jeannie Maud in 1912, one of the first women to be elected to the church assembly. This was the year in which the church acquired a new organ to replace the Vowles which was installed in 1865, in turn a replacement for the Harris and Byfield organ of 1726. The new organ was built by the famous makers Harrison and Harrison in Durham. It had four keyboards and 71 speaking stops. The largest pipe was 32 feet long, the smallest a fraction of an inch. There were 4,350 pipes in all.

In 1912 a tabby kitten appeared at the door to the south ambulatory, attracted by the sound of the organ played by Ralph Morgan. For fifteen years the cat would be a local celebrity, the verger Eli Richards taking special care of him. He was named Tom. He kept down the numbers of mice and pigeons which were always congregating in the church grounds and he buried their remains in a galvanised bath kept for him beneath the altar. Tom would always attend choir practice and would sit serenely next to the organist on an organ stool. He attended more church services than the clergy and during the sermon he liked to sit on the favoured lap of one of the congregation. When he died in 1927 he was given a grand funeral. His tiny coffin was carried to the churchyard by the verger and the vicar and he was buried in hallowed ground.

Vicar John Bateman-Champain's incumbency coincided very closely with that of the church cat. He was a keen cricketer. 'Where is the vicar?', asked Jeannie the wife of Bob Mortimer the curate (who later became the Bishop of Exeter). 'You know where he is', was the reply. 'He's playing cricket. Go and fetch him.'[1] In 1920 the cricket eleven came top of the second division of the Bristol Central League winning ten out of their twelve matches. In 1921 the St Mary's eleven finished near the top of the first division of the league and the second eleven finished runners up in division three. There was also a third eleven but they played only a few matches. St Mary's also ran three association football clubs. In 1920 the first team played in the second division of

the Church of England league, with a second team in the third division and Redcliffe Athletic in division four.[2]

It fell to John Bateman-Champain to guide St Mary Redcliffe through World War I. In 1914-18 there was little action at home but the soldiers were suffering terrible bombardments in the trenches of Flanders and on the borders of France and Germany. Hardly a family escaped without the loss of a loved one in the trench war-fare. The men who had left so cheerfully at the beginning of the war came home tired, saddened and disillusioned after the loss of so many lives. The problem was exacer-bated by the greatest flu epidemic of all time which, in the final year of the war, carried off more lives than the years of heavy bombardment in the trenches.

The 1920s began with hope. The Great War after all was seen as the war to end all wars. In 1928 John Bateman-Champain was succeeded by Edward L A Hertslet who was known to his friends by his initials as 'Elah'. The parish of St Mary Redcliffe enjoyed the innocent peace of the twenties but the youth of the parish still had to understand something about military matters. The parish magazine of the time describes the inspection of the Church Lads Brigade. The day fixed for this annual event was 22 June. The inspecting officer, General Lord Methuen, arrived at Temple Meads station at three o'clock where he was met by the regimental colonel, the son of

The Harrison and Harrison organ: a view of the organ pipes in the clerestory.

Opposite: the console showing the stops and four keyboards.

Tom the cat lived through World War I and died in 1927. He was so popular with the congregation that he was buried in sacred ground.

the Rev. John Maud who had been vicar before the war, and by a guard of honour under the command of Captain Came. After a lunch with Sir George White of the Bristol Aircraft Company Lord Methuen was driven with the vicar, Canon Hertslet and Colonel Chester Master to Redcliffe church where some time was spent looking over the building. Then the lads were inspected:

> Punctually at 5 o'clock the battalion under the command of Major Sefton Clark, was drawn up in the gardens in readiness to receive the general who arrived immediately after. Having inspected the lines and witnessed the usual ceremonial drill, which was excellently performed, General Methuen complimented the lads on their work, and then said that he was pleased to know that the qualifications for membership of the Church Lads Brigade were very stringent. Quality was more to be desired than quantity. He would far rather see 300 lads well turned out than double the number of boys somewhat rough and not such good company...[3]

In 1930 Canon Hertslet attended the Lambeth conference and he returned well pleased with the proceedings. He had made many contacts at Lambeth and he had spoken with clerics from the Commonwealth countries and Christian people from all over the world. A new set of embroideries had been made for the Trinity season. There was a green altar frontal designed by William Morris representing a bed of growing Madonna lilies. The other vestures were also embroidered with the flowers of Our

Lady to match the altar covering. The amount of needlework in the embroidery was prodigious but the ladies responsible did not wish to be named. The vicar knew that one of his congregation was the only person in the world who could have produced such work so speedily and so perfectly. This lady was Mrs Roderick Fry; very professional in her work, she studied ancient designs and used directional stitches. She would go to great lengths to get the right material and thread for her embroideries. When Elah wrote his December letter in the church magazine it was on a hopeful note:

John Primatt Maud, vicar 1904-1911.

My Dear People,

Before this letter is in your hands the 'Annus Mirabilis' will have passed into history. 1930 has been indeed a 'Marvellous Year' for us in Redcliffe. And as we look back over its outstanding events, we may well close it with our hearts' deepest Te Deum for its record of God's graciousness towards us. It has seen the happiness of the great family gathering, of which the stimulus and the echoes still abide; the glorious gift for the church's restoration; the coming of the lovely embroideries which have enriched the sanctuary; the launching of the scheme for the reparation of the Parish Room: the extinction of the debt upon the Institute; the solution of the future of the Athletic Ground.[4]

Canon Hertslet went on to mention some of the many people he had met and heard at the Lambeth conference, a gathering which was truly international. They included the Bishops of Calcutta, of Chora Nagpur, Qu'Appelle, Bloemfontein, North Queensland, and Waikato. He met the Archdeacon of Palestine and a Mr Gill, the Dean of Johannesburg. He mentioned the Chancellor of Grahamstown, Father Winslow, and Miss Dorothy Ward, who in turn linked the church with the needs and claims of India,

Edward Louis Augustine Hertslet, vicar 1928-1937.

Canada, Australia, New Zealand, South Africa, and also the dispersions of Islam and the Jewish people. The canon had travelled much further than Lambeth, he had also managed to visit the Holy Land that year. 'I can never be thankful enough for the privilege and the education of spending Holy Week and Easter in the Holy Land,' he wrote.

The Church Lads Brigade was not the only youth movement at St Mary's. The Boy Scouts and the Girl Guides were flourishing in the thirties and the parish magazine gives excellent accounts of their summer camps and their outings.

The 1930s saw the great depression, the general strike, widespread unemployment and the dole queue. The last coal mine in Bedminster closed in 1936 and amongst the retired miners was Charlie Gill Miner who worked for 31 years in the mines. He went on to become Lord Mayor of Bristol in 1947. It was good that the grim era of mining coal from deep passages under the ground had at least passed in Bedminster but it was a tragedy that the closure was one of the many causes of unemployment during the great recession. A guest house was opened in Phippin Street to accommodate the unemployed. Simple meals were provided.

It was August 1939. The memory of the Great War of 1914-18 remained all too vivid for those who had survived it and those who had lost relatives and friends in the conflict. After the happy decade of the twenties and the unemployment of the thirties, the unthinkable had happened and Europe stood again on the brink of another war with Germany. In the vicarage of St Mary Redcliffe Canon Swann, who had succeeded Canon Hertslet in 1937, prepared a letter to his parishioners:

Dear friends of Redcliffe,

This is being written on Wednesday August the 30th when issues of peace and war are still undecided. There is still hope. As one of the lessons this morning put it 'almost hoping against hope' but while hope remains, the possibility of war is such that I must speak my mind about what seems to me to be the Christian attitude to this war, should it come…[5]

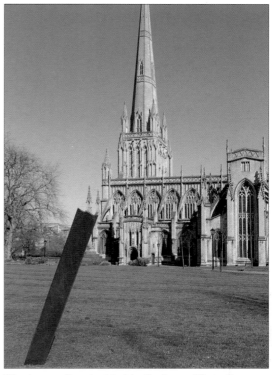

The tram rail embedded in the lawn. The rail remains where it struck, on Good Friday 1941, to remind people of the blitz.

But the war could not be averted and by the end of September the country was at war again. This time the German air power was such that they could strike right at the heart of British cities and in the following two years Bristol suffered terrible bombing raids from the Luftwaffe.

The undercroft was built soon after the outbreak of the war, to the plans of the architect Sir George Oatley who designed the university tower at the top of Park Street. A deep bunker was excavated to give shelter to hundreds of people. Inside the undercroft were pillars and stone vaulting like a church crypt, it was to prove a safe and cosy retreat during the air raids. It was necessary to rebuild the steps up to the north porch, and there is some uncertainty about what the steps were like before Oatley's reconstruction. Visitors from as early as Camden in 1586 had praised the beautiful flight of steps up to the porch. Before the war there were stone balustrades and sweeping curves leading up to the entrance and it is possible that the grand flight of steps had lasted since Tudor times. An illustration from Britton, published in 1813, shows the steps at their full development at that time, sweeping down in a widening flight from the north porch to a large square podium then down two grand flights to the west with stone balustrades on both sides. At Redcliffe Hill three grand flights of steps climbed up past the tower to give access to the church gardens on the south.

The first time the church came under threat from incendiaries was on the freezing cold night of 3 January 1941. The Vicar found a number of incendiaries burning in the churchyard but far more serious were those that had fallen on the roof of the church:

> ... He put out the incendiaries in the churchyard and ran up to the roof where he found a number burning. All the water in the buckets was frozen solid by the deep frost. Some incendiaries he threw clear of the building and some he kicked onto the lead roof to prevent them burning through... He then noticed smoke coming from a lower roof near the north porch and he went down to get water in case any further incendiaries fell. He found the water tank in the churchyard frozen. He succeeded in breaking the ice by jumping on it. Several buckets full of water were carried up to the roof. The vicar then noticed smoke coming from the aisle roof near the north porch. Three youths appeared in the churchyard. They were shown the way to the roof and promptly got to work and reported that they had extinguished the smouldering fire in a corner of the roofing.[6]

Canon Swann also remembered Good Friday, 11 April, 1941. This was the only occasion that a really large bomb fell on Redcliffe parish although of course there were very many smaller bombs and many incendiaries. He was in the undercroft when the big bomb landed, the very foundations of the undercroft rocked perilously with the thunderous explosion. It was followed by the horrifying sound of the endless falling of stones and debris. 'A direct hit on the church', he thought. 'Those are the roof and walls falling'. It is hard to imagine the fear and trepidation which he must have felt when he went up the steps in the darkness from the undercroft to the church, fully expecting to find that the site of 800 years of worship had been reduced to rubble. He entered the church. He looked all around. His prayers were answered. A miracle had taken place. In the darkness, to his astonishment and infinite relief, he could see no damage to the fabric. It was only when he went out through the south porch that he saw that houses on Redcliffe Hill had been reduced to a pile of rubble. There was nobody in sight but he could see that something was embedded in the lawn. It was part of a tramline that had somehow been thrown right over the doctor's house on the corner of Colston Parade and landed like a javelin spiked into the grass. He had no idea how high it had been thrown into the air. His thoughts were that the rail must remain. It would be of interest to future generations.

On another occasion, after a particularly severe blitz, Canon Swann received a simple and moving letter from a Redcliffe resident. He published it in the parish magazine for all to read:

> Dear Sir
>
> At about 2am on Monday my wife wondered if her beloved St Mary Redcliffe was still standing. We are Methodists by the way, but you will understand. I went to the door and called her. We shall never forget what we then saw. Against a background of lurid red the steeple with its heavenward pointing finger, shone like a beacon of hope. It stood and stands as all it signifies will stand, when dictators are an evil memory, and their works perished.
>
> This letter needs no acknowledgement but it may in some way serve to hearten and encourage you in the work you are doing, and amid the heartbreak of which you must see so much.
>
> Yours faithfully
>
> W M Picken[7]

Fry's House of Mercy was almost destroyed by the enemy action of January 1941. St Mary Redcliffe was very fortunate, for Temple Church became a victim of the blitz, as did the parish church of Clifton and many others in Bristol. St John's at Bedminster was also bombed. This was a particularly sad blow to St Mary Redcliffe for St John's was the mother church. The ruins of St John's Bedminster were retained for a long time after the bombing but in 1967 it had to be demolished. The only relic to be saved was the Norman font which came to St Mary's.

In 1942 Redcliffe was on the air when radio broadcasts were transmitted from eleven o'clock for fifteen minutes to the armed forces on the four Sundays in August. The air raids became less and less frequent after the Battle of Britain but the war dragged on for nearly six years. At long last, in May 1945, came the news that every person had been waiting so long to hear:

> None of us will forget Tuesday May 8th, even the sun shone brightly on VE Day, and there must have been very few citizens of Redcliffe who did not go down on their knees and thank God that, in Europe at least, the war was over. The streets were gay with red white and blue bunting, and flags, whilst here and there, we saw

the hammer and sickle of the USSR and the stars and stripes of the USA. In the parish church there were two celebrations of Holy Communion, at 8am and 9.30am both well attended, considering how short and surprising was the notice of VE day given. Services of thanksgiving and peace were held at 11am noon and 7.30 pm and a very large majority of parishioners came to give thanks. Throughout the day people from all parts of the city came into the church for a few moments of private prayer and mediation – one of the most notable features was the number of families which came together, a rare sight these days. We remember the delightful picture of a young woman with three very small children, too young to know quite what to say as they went down upon their knees, but so lovingly instructed by their mother.[8]

VE Day, 8 May 1945, was the greatest party of all time. Every city, town and village in the country celebrated all through the night. The pent-up emotions of six long years broke out and there was singing and dancing in the streets, the pubs and the parks. But there was still a dignity and order about the joyfulness. Many had not forgotten that in the Far East men of many nations were still fighting and dying. In many parts of Europe too there were many starving people and shattered lives. There were mothers, wives and children whose joy was tempered by personal tragedy.

1.   Richard F Cartwright
2.   PM 1920 and 1921
3.   PM Sept 1929
4.   PM Dec 1930
5.   PM Sept 1939
6.   CS 2004
7.   PM 1941
8.   PM June 1945

CHAPTER TWELVE

A Royal Visit

One unfortunate loss during the war years was the Mission Church at Barnard's Place on the New Cut. The church was closed for economic reasons after the recession of the 1930s but the infant school, which did such a valuable job for the children of Redcliffe, continued until well after the war and was moved to Windmill Hill in about 1958.

The war was over but there were still shortages. Food was rationed and luxury items were scarce but the economy was recovering very quickly. There were major changes in health and education. Only a few were wealthy enough to run a car but there were some compensations. The television set, which before the war was the preserve of a few wealthy households in the London area, was now available at more modest prices and broadcasts were made in all the major centres. Television was a novelty that was greatly enjoyed by young and old.

Alongside innovation, the old customs prevailed and in 1949, only a few months away from the middle of the century, parishioners were urged to go on the pipe walk:

> Make a note in your diary of Sat Oct 8th. We meet at the Redcliffe Hill gate of the church at 2.30pm and follow the line of the conduit to its source at Knowle. This is an annual event and nobody can account themselves true members of Redcliffe unless they have been on the pipe walks and taken part in the attendant ceremonies. Have you been? If so why not come again? Let this year's walk be the best ever. The time taken is about 1 $^1/_2$ hours.[1]

The parish magazine of July 1952 contained a hilarious report of the choir outing to the river Wye on 10 June. The participants assembled at 7.15 in the morning.

> Mr Pugsley had given a typed program of clear details weeks before but he took no chances of us being late and phoned us all to drag us out of bed. We had coffee at Tintern. The crew proved mutinous and before long the passengers had taken over steering. (Isn't it odd that folk who had difficulty in finding their way through music

could navigate the Wye so successfully!) Mr Rigg showed interest in salmon fishing, excitement was high as he cast his line and almost immediately there was a great shout as he hauled to the surface a silver salmon weighing ten pound or so. Later the fish was found to show signs of having been caught before. And it as an odd coincidence that there was another salmon on board and enough brown paper to wrap both fish in. Each fish was cut into five pieces and lots drawn so that some of us could take home two pounds of fish each.[2]

The Queen's entrance to the church in 1956 with Richard Cartwright, via the south-west path and south porch.

This was the year in which King George VI died, and the following year a very longstanding supporter of St Mary Redcliffe also died. She was Nurse Frances Elizabeth Friend (1871-1953), a pioneer hospital-trained nurse who gave her life to tending sick parishioners. Nurse Friend was the third in a succession of five nurses and devoted church-women who served Redcliffe in the capacity of parish nurse. She retired from her full-time job in 1910 aged 39 but she still did a lot for the sick and she enjoyed a further 43 years living in the parish.

The death of the king meant that the new Elizabethan era had begun. In 1953 there was to be a coronation for the young queen. Malcolm Neil Tanner of St Mary Redcliffe was one of twenty choirboys selected to go to Westminster Abbey and sing at the coronation. He remembered having to rise at 3.45 am on the great day and sitting in the abbey sucking glucose sweets to sooth his throat. Many went to London to see the coronation but the majority had to make do with the television set and the street parties that were organised for the children.

Coronation Day was a very memorable and happy one. Nearly two hundred people came to Holy Communion and thereafter we imagine that the entire parish and congregation are glued to its radio and TV set! The editors tore themselves away (a little reluctantly we must admit!) soon after two o'clock and were soon happily embroiled in the various highly successful street parties. It was rather sad that so many were driven indoors by rain, but spirits did not seem to be noticeably dampened. The ringers rang a full peal during the afternoon. In the evening there was country and Morris dancing in the churchyard. A surprisingly large number of people turned out, considering the arctic conditions. However, it did at least encourage people to join in the dancing, if only to restore their circulation. As darkness fell we were able to enjoy and admire the sight of the west front of the church bathed in golden light.[3]

The Queen and Richard Cartwright on the steps of the north porch, 1956.

The Queen made a royal tour of the whole country at the time of the coronation, but her visit to St Mary Redcliffe was made three years later, in April 1956. Many could not help but to compare the visit with that of Queen Elizabeth I nearly 400 years earlier. When the great day dawned the weather was fair and the crowd outside St Mary Redcliffe had already swollen to an estimated twenty thousand. There had been nothing to compare with the royal visit since the placing of the capstone in 1872 and only a few octogenarians survived to tell of that famous occasion. The rooftops were covered with those who wanted a better view. School was cancelled but every child was present in the churchyard clutching a union jack and lining the route which the queen would take. The children practised their cheering and flag waving but there was no need to practise, the joy and enthusiasm was all there in great abundance. A signal was transmitted from Temple Meads station. The royal train had arrived on time and her majesty Queen Elizabeth II was on her way to St Mary Redcliffe. Suddenly the church bells of St Mary Redcliffe were ringing out their 'grandsire cinques' loud and clear across the whole of Bristol.

It was 382 years since Queen Elizabeth I had seen the church at Redcliffe. Would our new queen be quite so impressed as her predecessor had been? There was cheering from all quarters as the royal car made its approach. It had been decided that the

A crowd on Redcliffe Hill as the Queen approaches the car for the next stage of her royal visit.

Queen should enter the church from the west door rather than the north porch, this was so that she could make a processional route through the church gardens and have a grand exit through the north porch where she could wave and be seen by the crowd from her high vantage point. The Queen was escorted by the vicar, the Rev. Richard Cartwright, and the Duke followed behind with the Lord Mayor and other dignitaries. The path through the gardens was lined solidly with children, every child waving a union jack and carrying a very wide smile. It was slow progress for the Queen wanted to acknowledge the younger children:

As the open car with the queen and the duke made its way slowly around the church from Redcliffe Way and up Redcliffe Hill the crowd gave them a tremendous reception. The sun was shining as the royal couple stepped from the car and walked the few yards inside the gate. The lord mayor presented the vicar to the queen and the duke and then Mr M G Meade-King (churchwarden) and Mr J Baldwin (junior church warden) and Mr E Richards (verger). On the south lawn were children of Redcliffe and Temple Colston schools and they were only two or three yards from the royal couple as they passed along the drive some sixty yards to the church which they entered by the west door. These children made the most of their good fortune in having such a favoured position and the queen smiled her pleasure as they cheered and waved flags. Just before the queen arrived they had practised their cheering and flag waving as the vicar and his party came from the church to take up their positions at the south west gate. Redcliffe Boys also lined the pathway within the balustrade on Redcliffe Hill while, as the queen and the duke walked to the west door, they paused to take special notice of the infants lined up against the south wall. There were nearly two hundred, among them three Polish children in embroidered costumes. Altogether some 900 children were in the church precincts on the south west side.[4]

Inside the west door the royal party had the first glimpse down the glory of the nave. Then they saw the wonder of the changing pattern of the pillars and the arches. They saw the stained glass and the window traceries as they walked down the aisles and the transepts. Sunshine lit the windows and they saw the altar bathed in soft light. The church itself was at its best with altar decorations and the beautiful floral patterns including the Madonna lilies embroidered by the late Mrs Roderick Fry. Among the treasures which the Queen and the Duke saw were the letters patent which Elizabeth I granted in 1571 for the setting up of a free grammar school in the Chapel of the Holy Spirit. Only a memorial cross occupied the site of the chapel but Redcliffe Church had survived the centuries of change and progress. Other sights inspected by the Queen and Duke included examples of the vestments which proved to be of great interest to the Queen. They were shown the tomb of William Canynges and the armour of Admiral Sir William Penn, father of the founder of Pennsylvania. They were shown the whalebone and they were told the story of John Cabot and his ship the *Matthew*. Before the royal party left the church, the Queen and the Duke signed the visitors' book and the Queen was impressed to find that it had once been signed by her grandmother, Queen Mary.

The Rt. Rev. Richard Fox Cartwright remembered that the Queen particularly liked William Penn's armour and the Canynges tomb but she was not impressed by the heavy Victorian reredos that obstructed the view of the east end of the church. The Duke of Edinburgh was very critical of the red tile flooring which he felt was quite out of keeping with the rest of the church. The departure, after only fifteen minutes inside the church, gave the crowds on the north side of the church the opportunity they had been waiting for. They had a wonderful view of the Queen and Duke as they made their way slowly down the steps on the long approach to their car. The royal party paused to look back and gaze up at the stately spire and the vicar pointed out features of the building. As the royal procession moved on the crowd cheered enthusiastically and hundreds of flags were waving. At this point the bells sounded out again, ringing a 'querris' and another short touch of 'cinques'.

'I thank you for showing us your lovely church', said the Queen as she left. It may not have been as gushing as her predecessor's remarks, but she had an impossible act to follow. It was an honest and appropriate tribute.

The Rt. Rev. Richard Cartwright, who had the good fortune to escort the queen, had moved into the vicarage on New Year's Eve 1951. He described the area around the vicarage in Redcliffe Parade East at the middle of the twentieth century. This once fashionable part of Redcliffe had fallen a little in the social scale:

> Before we leave the vicarage some memories of the lane at the back. On the vicarage side were, for the most part, what had become garages, though at number nine Mr Anthony had his sweets to supply his shop ranged in shelves all round: but on the south side were stables and cottages: in one of these Mr Cole kept his horse. Every morning he would come immaculate in polished gaiters, harness his horse and set out on his coal round. Later by somewhat devious means, the hospital bought all the buildings on the south side and built the hospital boiler house. For many years this was a nuisance: it belched forth black smoke. On all our south window sills we had to have glass tell tales, to measure the filthy emission. In the end we won.[5]

The morning after Richard Cartwright moved into the vicarage was New Year's Day 1952 and he arrived in time for the 8 am Eucharist. He went to the south porch to find

Older members of the congregation remember the second Victorian reredos, designed by George Godwin and carved in Caen stone by William Rice. Now in the Church of the Incarnation, Morrisville, Pennsylvania. Many complained that the reredos destroyed the view of the east end of the church.

it locked, then he went to the north porch which was also locked. Eventually he found a little door leading into the south ambulatory. Expecting the church to be empty he discovered a small congregation waiting in the Lady Chapel but with no priest to conduct the service. The curate arrived at ten past eight. One of the new vicar's first jobs was to make sure that this did not happen again.

The boundaries of Redcliffe Parish had already been extended to include part of Temple Parish and during an incumbency which lasted for twenty years Richard Cartwright saw two more boundary changes take in part of St John's Bedminster and also part of St Thomas's near Bristol Bridge.

Three years after the royal visit work began on replacing the windows in the Lady Chapel which had been damaged beyond repair by a bomb blast during the war. Mr H J Stammers was both the designer and the contractor for this work. On the north side he designed the Magnificat window and the Annunciation with a red-winged Gabriel telling Mary that she would bear a child. On the south side is depicted a scene from the childhood of Jesus when his parents found him in the temple at Jerusalem questioning the religious leaders and the lawyers of the times. The finest window is at the

The Magnificat window by Harry Stammers of York. The centre piece, shown, depicts the virgin with child.

Opposite top: The Pentacost window is another fine example of stained glass work at St Mary Redcliffe.

Opposite below: The east window of the Lady Chapel is a noteworthy twentieth-century addition. It was designed and crafted in the 1960s by Harry Stammers.

east window of the church with its yellows and reds dominating the space above the Lady Chapel screen. It shows the nativity scene with shepherds to the left and the finely robed Magi to the right. The child looks up at his mother from the manger and Joseph stands watching a few feet away.

The crossing at this time was dominated by the great Victorian reredos, built from Caen stone and completed in 1870. Previous vicars had tried in vain to remove it but this was no easy matter for so large an object and it seemed sacrilege to destroy something for which the Victorians had paid a thousand pounds. After advertising the reredos for sale in both America and Canada, a solution was found. The Church of the Incarnation at Morrisville in Pennsylvania agreed to have it. This was very fitting because Morrisville was the nearest church to the manor house of William Penn the Younger. The great reredos was carefully packed and shipped off to its new home in America. When the reredos was gone there followed discussions about what to put in its place but in the end the congregation decided on the cheapest and simplest of

all solutions. Without the reredos they could see the Lady Chapel for the first time and more significantly the beautiful east window – it had all been hidden before. They wanted nothing but a better view of the east end of their church.

Fragments of the medieval glass can be seen in St John's Chapel where the windows were restored in the nineteenth century. The chapel became the resting place for the old Norman font of St John's Bedminster (the font had been found in a garden used as a flower pot). To accommodate the growing number of visitors from America St John's also became the American chapel, its restoration was enabled by Friends of St Mary Redcliffe in the United States of America. The kneelers depict the arms of the thirteen original states and the seven original dioceses. They had all been worked by individual American friends.

1. PM Oct 1949
2. PM July 1952
3. PM Jun 1953
4. PM May 1956
5. Richard F Cartwright

CHAPTER THIRTEEN

Towards 2000

On 26 November 1967 Miss Ethel Francombe died. In her later life she lived in Colston Parade with her sister where the two elderly ladies were a familiar sight with their large hats and parasols. She has already been mentioned earlier in this history with her wonderful account of the children's outing to Weston-super-Mare in 1895. Her roots and memories went back well into the nineteenth century and her links with St Mary Redcliffe went back even further. Her grandfather, who was a freeman of Bristol, had fought under the Duke of Wellington in the Peninsular Wars. There may be a generation accidentally missing from the obituary in the parish magazine but according to the account he fought under Nelson at the Battle of the Nile. Ethel's father, James Thomas Francombe was born in 1833 at Redcliffe Hill. He was educated at the Boys' Blue School in Pile Street and he became the headmaster of the Redcliffe Endowed Boys' School from 1872 until 1909. When Redcliffe was redeveloped after the war a block of flats was named after him and Ethel was thrilled by this tribute to her father. A house in the new school was also named after him.

During the war Miss Francombe, when in her sixties and seventies, helped with the sick and the elderly and she was responsible for running the relief committee. Working with her sister May, she ran a temporary hostel at the hall in the Wills factory for those who had lost their homes in the bombing. She served for forty years on the Parochial Parish Council. She lived just long enough to see the new Secondary School opened at Redcliffe in 1967. The school was co-educational, combining the Redcliffe Boys' School with Temple Colston Girls'.[1]

The pressure for places in the secondary school was very fierce. Admission to the school was governed by a very strict points system based on the children's place of residence and on church attendance; only by this means could any fair scheme be worked out. A proposal was put forward that at some future date it would be wise to enlarge the school to have an entry at sixth-form level. This was the year in which the Chatterton memorial was removed. It had stood outside the church for over a hundred years, Chatterton (it was then firmly believed) had committed suicide and for this reason the Victorians would not have his memorial in the church. The memorial was

The Rush Sunday tradition dates back 500 years. Note the rushes strewn in the aisle and the red robes of the civic dignitaries of Bristol on the right.

replaced with a slate plaque situated inside the church.

In 1969 Redcliffe Hill was widened to accommodate more traffic. This was not really a positive move for the church, as it drew more traffic into the area but there was a small consolation when the improvement plans included a balustraded walk on the west of the church. The following year there was a minor problem when the lease on the Church Hall ran out. It was resolved to build a new hall on the east side of Pump Lane and the optimistic deadline of the end of the year was set as a target date to complete the building. In the meantime Townsend House and the Methodist Church hall were used to help out with regular meetings. In June 1970 the scouts and cubs met at St Luke's church hall with Reg Taylor and Bob Everett as the leaders of a thriving troop. In July 1969 St Luke's Junior and Infants School was transferred to the St Mary Redcliffe Junior and Infant School. The buildings at Windmill Hill were shared between Redcliffe children and the Holy Cross Roman Catholic School. Holy Cross acquired their own new buildings and the Redcliffe children were able to spread into the part of the building formerly used by them.

In January 1971 Richard Cartwright, in his twentieth year as vicar, wrote in the parish magazine about the changes in Redcliffe. He identified what has become a growing problem, namely that more and more of the congregation did not actually live in the parish. This was seen as a good trend in the sense that new arrivals to Bristol were drawn to a famous and beautiful church but it had the inevitable drawback that the newcomers were not always familiar with happenings in the area around the church. Redcliffe was becoming less of a parish church. He went on to describe the recent changes such as the balustraded walk along the side of the churchyard which was 'completed and beautiful'. The old Hope & Anchor Hotel, which had been damaged during the war, and also Mulletts Garage together with the warehouse which adjoined Dr Jenkins's house had been demolished and a large new block was in the course of erection by Bristol Municipal Charities. On the other side of Redcliffe Hill all the shops except for three single story frontages had gone, the church hall had also gone and so had the old Boys' school and the buildings in Jubilee Place. The only thing that remained was the plane tree which used to stand in front of the former vicarage. The contractors were levelling the site for a large new office block with some housing and a shopping precinct.[2]

This year (1971) was a very successful one for the choir. They were invited to sing at the services in Canterbury cathedral throughout the month of August and to sing at evensong every day. But another highlight of the year was the choir football team, the best ever at St Mary Redcliffe. They played against St Mary Yate and according to the report Yate played good football and it was quite a tough match. This is hard to believe when the score was twelve goals to one for St Mary Redcliffe! The team beat Bristol Cathedral twice and Christ Church Clifton by seven goals to two. St Albans at Westbury Park were beaten five-two and they drew 4-4 with Redcliffe United.[3]

Rev. Canon Kenneth Clark was appointed vicar in 1972. He arrived at Redcliffe with his wife Elizabeth and after only three days he became involved in a debate about the future of the organ. He was instrumental in the decision to restore and enlarge the existing instrument. He was also active in installing a public address system in the church and the upgrading of the central heating system. In 1974 he helped to organise two services, one at Westbury-on-Trym and the other at St Mary Redcliffe to mark the five-hundredth anniversary of the death of William Canynges. He guided the church through the new Alternative Service Book which appeared in the 1970s, and he was very active in church societies. In 1982 he became Archdeacon of Swindon.

Kenneth Clark was followed by the Rev. David Frayne. He came with his family from the parish of Caterham in Kent where he began his ministry as a Deacon and rose to become Canon Emeritus at Southwark Cathedral. David Frayne, like his predecessor, served Redcliffe for just over a decade. He helped to invigorate the youth movements and he was very active in trying to reduce the traffic around the church. His wife was active in the Mothers' Union. He wrote to the Canynges Society:

> I regard as very important that people come to know and love their parish churches – and in this case St Mary Redcliffe – in a variety of ways. Because through them there are a great variety of ways in which folk can be led towards an enrichment of their lives. Those of you who are members of the Canynges Society continue to enable the very structure and beauty of this well known building to tell (as some have described it) of the 'gospel in stone' – not forgetting the magnificence of the stained glass and the music which Redcliffe offers in addition to regular acts of worship.
>
> The undercroft is now adding a new enrichment to occasions when people meet

together. Having played its part in the restoration of the interior, the Parochial Church Council is now engaged in the talks of refurnishing. When this is complete much hope is that the undercroft will become more publicly known and appreciated. It certainly deserves to be...[4]

He was right concerning the future of the undercroft. It became a venue for many societies, most importantly it provided a focus for the youth of the parish to congregate. The Blue Notes Jazz band became the resident group and on Wednesday nights the youth of Redcliffe jived and gyrated to the sound of their music. Amongst the jivers were members of Chatterton's Mob, the trendy youth club which met every Friday. The undercroft also became a coffee bar and a meeting place for residents and visitors to have snacks and refreshments during the day. There is a lovely memorial in the undercroft to Roger Bennett, leader of the Blue Notes and a much-loved BBC Radio Bristol broadcaster.

In 1988 David Frayne had to organise a royal visit when Princess Anne visited St Mary Redcliffe on the occasion of the opening of Townsend House. An exhibition showing much of the church history was displayed in the Lady Chapel. In 1993 Tony Whatmough became vicar and a few years later he too had to organise a royal visit, this time from the Queen. In contrast to the Queen's previous visit forty years earlier, she and the Duke of Edinburgh attended a service in the church and the details were worked out between St Mary's and Buckingham Palace. Tony Whatmough asked the Queen if she remembered her earlier visit to Redcliffe. 'St Mary Redcliffe is not the kind of church one forgets once one has visited it', was her comment as she signed the book in St John's chapel. Other royal visits had included Princess Margaret in October 1965 and Princess Marina the Duchess of Kent, 1957.

In 1997 there came a novel addition to the exhibits at St Mary Redcliffe. It was a scientific rather than a religious or historical display. The chaotic pendulum looks rather like a pendulum but it does not swing to and fro in a regular manner. On the contrary, its future motion is totally unpredictable. The effect is achieved by constructing the pendulum out of metal pipes in such a fashion that the pipes fill with water from a supply near the point of suspension and, as the pendulum moves to left or right, the lower arm fills with water. The motion of the pendulum is chaotic, it is impossible to predict where it will be in one minute's time. It leaves the visitor with the

This modern icon in the Sanctuary is by Peter Murphy. It shows the Virgin Mary in the centre panel; St Nicholas and St Stephen are on the left and St Catherine and St George are on the right. All four saints had chapels dedicated to them in St Mary Redcliffe.

Below: The Garden of Remembrance.

thought that if we cannot predict the immediate future then it is impossible to predict anything in the future with any degree of certainty.

The last year of the millennium saw the sad sight of the last service at St Luke's Bedminster. A last thanksgiving service was held on Monday, 11 November. St Luke's was not one of the ancient churches of Bristol but it had served the area for 170 years and the closure was a sad reflection of falling church attendances and the population changes in the area. The same year saw a happier event when the Mothers' Union celebrated their centenary. Their first meeting at Redcliffe took place in 1899 but unfortunately records for the period before the war are missing. The longest serving enrolling member was Mrs Olive Pagett with 21 years to her credit. When she died the vicar's wife, Mrs Liz Frayne became the enrolling member. In 1947 a link was made with the Mothers' Union in Victoria, Australia and for the next half century a regular correspondence was kept up. In 1995 a link was established with Mbale in Uganda and again regular contact was maintained.

The new millennium saw the loss of several old friends of Redcliffe. On 6 December 2000 was held the funeral of Trevor Stanford, better known as Russ Conway, the 'King of the Keyboard'. Trevor was born in Bristol and he was encouraged in his musical career by the choirmaster Ralph Morgan. His number one hit *Side Saddle* was played at the end of the service.

In September 2001 died Gilbert Croker who had been born in 1908. Gilbert lived over fifty years in Bedminster and he was educated at the Redcliffe Endowed Boys' School. During the war Gilbert had served as a fireman and he was involved with the full force of the bombing. In 1999 the Queen presented him with Maundy money at Bristol Cathedral. After his wife had died in 1979 Gilbert moved to a flat in Colston Parade. One of his hobbies was writing poetry and he wrote of his beloved church:

> As I enter this holy place,
> Its silence envelopes me
> Which, from the noisy world outside
> Instantly sets me free.

In the same year died the senior vestryman Alec Stevens, who was nearly a hundred years old and had served Redcliffe for almost all his life. He was carried to the

Redcliffe Mission Church in his mother's arms in 1902 when she went for her Christmas communion and he died nearly a century later in June 2001. The school records showed that at the age of eight this future tireless church worker had been caned for laziness. Alec became churchwarden and he was a vestryman for over fifty years. He received his memorial in the Garden of Remembrance dedicated to him with his name cut on the remembrance stone, a large slab of Welsh slate.

The parish magazine for February 2002 tells of the greatest ever audience for a service at St Mary Redcliffe, if we include those watching on television:

> Those of us who raised their voices for the recording of this popular programme last month will be able to hear and see ourselves on BBC1 on February 11. Songs of Praise, now presented by former choir boy Aled Jones, regularly attracts an audience of five million people. The BBC will be back in church again – but this time microphones only – on Passion Sunday (April 1) to record evensong for transmission to the world service.[5]

One of the hymns sung was 'Glorious things of Thee are spoken' to the tune of 'Abbots Leigh'. The tune was very appropriate because it will be remembered that Abbots Leigh and St Mary Redcliffe were both originally part of the Berkeley estates.

At this time it was recognised that the church organ, built by the famous firm of Harrison and Harrison and installed in 1912, was in need of a major overhaul. The organ was described by William McVicker, the organ curator at the Royal Festival Hall, as 'the finest high-Romantic organ ever constructed.' The cost was estimated as £800,000 but a programme of restoration was put in place with completion in 2012 on the hundredth anniversary of its installation.

The choir outing of 2001/2002 was quite exceptional. No longer was the Wye Valley the venue for choir outings and even Canterbury was not far enough for them. The choir went to America. Leaving Heathrow after Christmas by jumbo jet they flew the Atlantic with their friends and relatives to visit the major American cities of New York and Washington. The Tavener 'God is with us' was wonderfully sung in four very different settings. They performed in a concert at Washington and in New York, they gave solos at the churches of St Thomas the Divine and Holy Trinity, both of them close to Ground Zero, the site of the nine-eleven tragedy when only three months

The chaotic pendulum is designed to stimulate our thoughts about the universe. It is impossible to predict its future motion. The Heisenberg uncertainty principle predicts similar results.

earlier the World Trade Centre was destroyed by terrorists. Whilst everybody in the party was very conscious of the tragedy they did not allow it to spoil the occasion. Among the sights were the Chrysler Building illuminated at night; other memories were the long queue to get to the top of the Empire State Building and the fear of going to the edge to take a photograph. The nights were cold in New York, there was no heating at the YMCA but one advantage was that they could enjoy skating on the frozen lake of Central Park. The most magical part of the trip was celebrating the New Year in the Park along with several hundred thousand others. They sang pop songs and traditional songs. They danced on Seventh Avenue wearing silly hats. Best of all was when the clocks struck midnight and they joined hands with 100,000 Americans as the British accents joined with the Americans' in a great rendering of *Auld Lang Syne*.

As we reach the end of the story there are many reminders of the cost of maintaining the highest standards at St Mary Redcliffe. In November 1996 a section of the choir clerestory fell into the ambulatory. Luckily nobody was hurt by the fall, but inspection of the fabric showed that major repairs were required to the stonework. All the clerestory windows had to be rebuilt and the cost was £800,000. This was followed by another major bill when uplighting was installed in the nave and the church was completely rewired.

There is, however, one story well worth telling that resulted in a great saving. It is

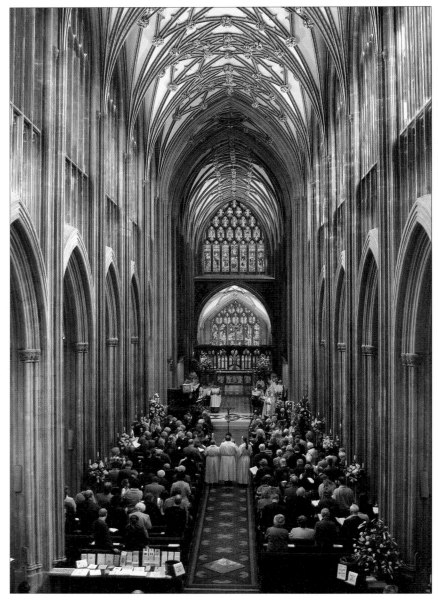

The nave of the church with the congregation gathered for the Easter Gospel.

Opposite: the new 'tower' is only 50cm tall but makes an effective firebreak.

that of the missing tower of St Mary Redcliffe. The story opens with the annual fire insurance premium, a hefty £60,000 a year. It was discovered that St Mary Redcliffe had to pay more in insurance than most cathedrals. The reason given was that it did not have a central tower at the crossover. A central tower, a common feature on many cathedrals, acts as a fire break so that if fire breaks out in the nave or transepts, then only one wing of the church would be destroyed. Without a central tower the fire is likely to spread to all four sections of the church.

Was there a solution to this problem? Why not build a tower on the crossover? It is one thing to build a tower from the ground but quite another to build one on what is effectively the roof of the church. And yet there was a solution. There was evidence that the fourteenth-century stonemasons knew about the dangers of fire. The four central pillars at the crossover had been constructed with a larger section than the pillars of the rest of the church – as if to support a tower above. The tower need only be a few metres tall and in fact a tower of one metre high was suggested. This satisfied the insurance company but not English Heritage. A compromise was reached and a tower of just 50 centimetres was designed. It satisfied both the insurance company and English Heritage. Thus did St Mary Redcliffe acquire a new tower, invisible from below but acting as a fire break above and saving the church some £20,000 or more in annual insurance premiums.

Finally the story moves to the Arctic Circle. John Pickard, the church warden, and his wife Sue were taking a cruise along the coast of Norway to the land of the midnight sun:

The sun was shining, the sea was calm and the 'Finnmarken' restaurant was almost full with happy holidaymakers of varied nationalities. I spied two empty places at a window table, at which an elderly gentleman and his much younger companion were sitting. After the usual courtesies of ascertaining that the places were indeed vacant, I sat down beside the gentleman, whereupon his companion, daughter or carer perhaps, got up to leave (I do sometime have this effect on people!) taking with her a small appetising bunch of grapes. The gentleman explained with some amusement that he had mistaken the very realistic plastic grapes for real ones and his daughter was returning them to the buffet table.

Then he enquired, as fellow countrymen do when on holiday, from which part of England did we come? When hearing 'Bristol' he asked 'which part?' I found this question somewhat surprising and enquired if he therefore knew Bristol. 'Oh yes!' he replied, 'I was vicar of St Mary Redcliffe for a number of years'. To say I was speechless was an understatement! I thought that I could not have heard correctly. I knew for certain he was not David Frayne, fairly certain that he was not Kenneth Clark, so who on earth...? As I mentally dressed him in a dog collar, the penny dropped – he was the Right Reverend Richard Fox Cartwright, former bishop of Plymouth, sitting next to me beyond the Arctic Circle, having lunch.[6]

Can there be any doubt that the name of St Mary Redcliffe extends to every corner of the Earth?

1. PM Oct 1967
2. PM Jan 1971
3. PM Apr 1971
4. CS 1992
5. PM Feb 2002
6. PM Oct 2002

CHAPTER FOURTEEN

The Nativity

It is Christmas Day. The great majority of families are at home with their children, exchanging greetings and opening presents. There are some, however, who are seated in the nave of the church watching an enactment of the very first Christmas Day from over two thousand years ago. The actors are inexperienced and unqualified. They are the youngest members of the congregation.

We see shepherds watching over their flock by night. The shepherds are amazed and astonished when they see an angel come down to visit them from heaven. They do not understand what they see until the angel tells the shepherds to have no fear for he brings them tidings of great joy. A new saviour is born this day in the nearby town of Bethlehem in Judea. The heavenly host appears and sings the praises of the new-born babe. The visions disappear and the shepherds chatter excitedly amongst themselves. They have been chosen to witness a wonderful event. They pen up their sheep and set off for Bethlehem to pay their respects to the new-born child.

The scene changes and we see kings and wise men travelling across the countryside. They have long robes, beards and crowns but bright young eyes sparkle from beneath the disguises. They point upwards to where the star of Bethlehem shines brightly high in the eastern sky. They travel onward to the east where they know they will come to the place where the child is born. Shepherds and kings arrive at a humble stable where the ox and the ass are joined by the sheep and the lamb. There in the stable are Mary and Joseph standing coy and proud and ready to welcome the worshippers. In the manger lies the young Jesus.

The children gather around the baby. There are more children than there are parts to play. This is a minor problem, easily solved by adding more angels for girls and extra lambs for the boys. When all the due respects have been paid the children line up to face their audience. Parents and grandparents crane their necks to get a glimpse of their own little ones. After a faltering and nervous start the children sing a Christmas carol. Shrill voices rise to the roof and echo from the vaulting. The sound is not as perfect and harmonious as the choir and many of the infants are unsure of the words. But their singing comes from the heart. It is simple and moving. It is executed with

Top: The Chatterton Mob. Most of them are about the same age as Thomas Chatterton in his prime.
Below: The wonderful sight of young people creating live music in the church.

A rare view of the nave without pews. They have been removed for floor maintenance.

little smiling faces. It is greatly appreciated by the audience. They all remember a time long ago when they too acted out the nativity and when they too were the youngest generation in the world.

Why then do we choose to end the narrative with a scene that should rightly appear right at the beginning? In the audience are grandparents who stood on the south lawn in the 1950s when they cheered and waved their flags on the Queen's visit half a century ago. The grandparents of these grandparents, when they were young, went on the church outing to the seaside described by Ethel Francombe in the 1890s. Every child has four grandparents and every child has sixteen grandparent's grandparents. But all around them is a history which goes back much further. Go back through the generations and if only we could trace them all we could find Chattertons amongst them. We would find Penns. We would find Cabots and Canynges. In the genes of the children we would find nearly all the people who have made St Mary's famous and many more who made their contribution. This is the past.

The children are the future.

BIBLIOGRAPHY

ABBREVIATIONS FOR GENERAL REFERENCES:

CS: Canynges Society

PM: St Mary Redcliffe Parish Magazine

BRO: Bristol Record Office

BOOKS, ETC:

Aughton: Peter Aughton: *Bristol, a People s History* (2000)

B&G: Transactions of the Bristol and Gloucestershire Archaeological Society

Bettey: J H Bettey: *Bristol Observed* (1986)

Brakspear: *St Mary Redcliffe Bristol* (B&G 1922)

Britton: John Britton: *An Architectural Essay relating to Redcliffe Church Bristol* (1813)

BRS: Bristol Record Society

Dresser and Giles: *Bristol and Transatlantic Slavery* (1999)

Drury: Michael Drury (Architects): St Mary Redcliffe Conservation Plan

Latimer XVI: John Latimer: *Annals of Bristol in the Sixteenth Century* (1908, reprinted 1970)

Latimer XVII: John Latimer: *Annals of Bristol in the Seventeenth Century* (1900, reprinted 1970)

Latimer XVIII: John Latimer: *Annals of Bristol in the Eighteenth Century* (1893, reprinted 1970)

Latimer XIX: John Latimer: *Annals of Bristol in the Nineteenth Century*
 (Part I 1897, Part II 1902, both reprinted 1970. Page numbers are Part I unless otherwise specified)

Little: Bryan Little: *The City and County of Bristol* (1954)

LRB: F B Bickley (ed): *The Little Red Book of Bristol* (1900) (Two volumes)

McInnes: C F McInnes: *A Gateway of Empire* (1939)

Neale: Frances Neale: *William Worcestre, The Topography of Medieval Bristol*, BRS Vol 51

Rikart: LT Smith: *Rikart s Kalendar*, Camden Society New Series, V, (1872)

Seyer: Samuel Seyer: *Memorials of Bristol* (Two Vols 1821-3)

Smith: Michael Quinton Smith: *St Mary Redcliffe* (1995)

Wilson: Ian Wilson: *The Columbus Myth* (1991)

INDEX